JOURNEY
TO
Ollantaytambo

Spring. '90

For Bill and Nancy,
With love and Best Wishes.
Ethan

JOURNEY TO

Ollantaytambo

*In the Sacred Valley
of the Incas*

ETHAN HUBBARD

Chelsea Green Publishing Company
Post Mills, Vermont

Rice in the bowl,
water in the pail;
how do you like these
uncommon miracles?

Setcho, in commenting
on Ummon's words
in the fiftieth Koan
of the Hekiganroku

Text and photographs copyright © 1990 by Ethan Hubbard
Printed in the United States of America

First printing, March 1990

Library of Congress Cataloging-in-Publication Data

Hubbard, Ethan, 1941–
    Journey to Ollantaytambo: in the sacred valley of the Incas / Ethan Hubbard.
        p. cm.
    ISBN 0-930031-28-8 (alk. paper): $16.95
    1. Cuzco Region (Peru)—Description and travel.   2. Ollantaytambo
(Peru)—Description.   3. Quecha Indians—Social life and customs.
    4. Hubbard, Ethan, 1941-   —Journeys—Peru—Cuzco Region.   I. Title.
F3611.C9H8   1990
918.5'3704633—dc20   89-77081
                                                                            CIP

To the memory
of Harry Smith

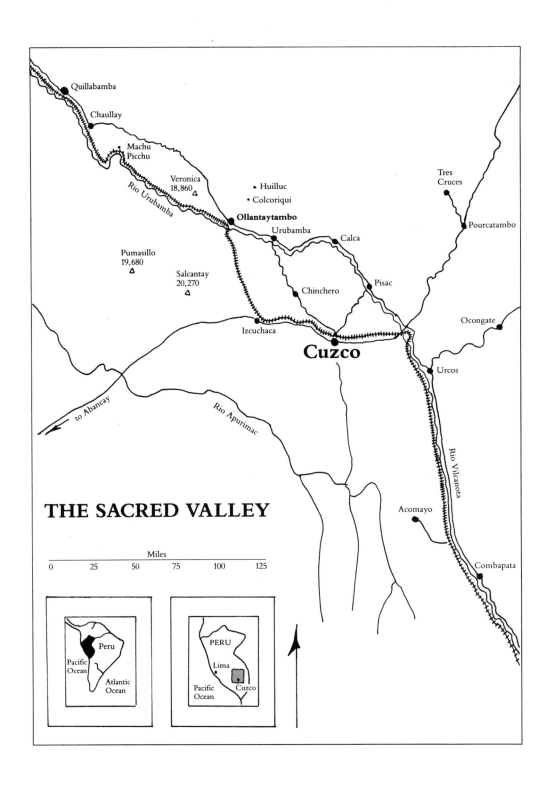

THE SACRED VALLEY

Miles

0   25   50   75   100   125

OR TEN YEARS NOW, I HAVE BEEN TRAVELING AND
photographing the people whose lives remind me
of what's truly important in the world. In 1987, a
chance encounter allowed me to see the TV documentary about Shirley MacLaine's spiritual adventures in Peru,
Out on a Limb. I knew immediately that I too must go to Peru
and invite further change into my life.

In New England where I live, I might go days with just a few
friendly people in my life: a visit along the road with my neighbors
as they let out their cows, some time with the regulars down at
the feed store, or perhaps a meal with a friend in town on a cold
winter's afternoon. Often I won't see anyone for days.

But when I throw myself out into remote villages for a month or more at a time, I am bombarded each day with encounters with the local people. It might be a visit with a shepherd in the mountains, a wedding dance after a fall harvest, perhaps a meal with an old bachelor by lamplight on the moor, and always the ragtag mob of children. By the end of the day, sometimes as many as five hundred people have come into my life. I thrive on it. Their friendship and greetings open up something within me, like a code, an opening that has never been fully tapped.

For me, the link with what Carlos Castaneda's Don Juan calls the *nagual*, the magic realm of the being, comes more alive in travel. Within me are shadowy dreams of being a Nepalese farmer in the Himalayas, a Mayan villager in the jungles of Guatemala, a Hebridean crofter on the outer islands of Scotland, and even an Australian Aborigine in the Outback. These came true a few years back; I told those adventures in my previous book, *First Light*.

Of late, I dream of being an Inca, one who rides a white horse through the mountains in the moonlight and watches eight sons planting corn in the shadows of the Temple of the Sun. Perhaps the *tonal*, what Castaneda calls the social part of our being, where 99.9 percent of the time we live (safely), exists only because we have forgotten how to dream, or how to live, or how to remember. Many of us have forgotten how to recall the ancient dreams that connect us, but millions are waking up, like seeds coming to life, waking up to who they really are.

Ethan Hubbard
Washington, Vermont
October 27, 1989

◆

CHAPTER ONE

I FLEW TO LIMA, THEN ON A SHORT FRIGHTENING TRIP ALONG THE ridge of the Andes to the high airport in Cuzco. Gazing down, I wonder whether my dream of trekking around a mountain named Ausangate, highly touted in guidebooks as being charged with spiritual energy, will materialize.

Cuzco is a city made entirely of the brown-red earth, its adobe and stone buildings climbing into the mountain landscape like gigantic sand castles. The city itself sits in a natural bowl amid the soaring mountain peaks, its brown-walled houses soft and earthy against the patchwork greens of the mountain slopes. "Cuzco" means "navel" in the local Quechua language. Indeed, there is a feeling, at least from the air, that this remains the center of a great territorial realm—mountains, jungle, desert, *altiplano*.

Five hundred years ago, when Incan civilization had been the most advanced society in all the Americas and perhaps the world, its lands stretched nearly three thousand miles, from Colombia in the north to Chile and Argentina in the south. This vast area included the jungles of the Amazon, a wild land the Incas called Antisuyo. From this very word came the Spanish nomenclature for the greatest mountain range of the continent, *Antis*, or as it came to be known, Andes.

A taxi takes me to a small hotel on a side street off the Plaza de Armas. I rest on and off in my room, adjusting mind, body, and soul to both jet lag and the altitude—at 11,150 feet—of one of the highest cities in the world. The staff at the hotel brings me innumerable cups of strong, almost bitter tasting coca tea, made from the same green leaves that produce cocaine. *Mate de coca* is one of the very best ways of fighting off altitude sickness, what these Quechua speakers call *soroche*.

That evening I wander down cobbled streets rubbing shoulders with city dwellers and country people. I eat in a small neighborhood restaurant with merchants and laborers, mostly men with rolled-up shirt sleeves, hunkered over their soup bowls with a tired hunger. I order *el menu*, trout, vegetables, bread, soup, and a dessert of fruit. It costs less than a dollar. The cashier, a short man with a dirty white apron tied about his upper body, asks if I wish to change money on the *mercado negro*, the black market. At first I am suspicious, but the cashier's countenance is benevolent and the trout was very good and my intuition says yes; I nod, and he carefully counts out my change in soiled and ripped Inti notes.

Near a centuries-old stone church in the San Francisco market, I watch a group of women dispensing hot food and drink to passersby. In the soft light of candles and cooking fires, they wear tall

white stovepipe hats and colorful skirts, their long black braids falling down below their waists. Their feet are dirty and gnarled, and only cheap rubber sandals protect them from the earth. Their food smells delicious in the cool night air, but I know the women have used unsafe water to wash their dishes and make their stews.

Cuzcueño men with large sacks throw down their cargoes at the feet of the women as if to say, "Here I am, old woman. Will you feed me, will you put me back together again?" These women wipe a fork with the edge of their dirty skirts and hand them to the men. Babies tied to the women's backs with colorful ponchos peer out with wide eyes at the night. A cat attempts to steal a fish from a skillet cooling on the ground, burns her paw, tries again, but cannot endure the hot oil and moves off disheartened. I glory in the simplicity of their lives.

The next morning, I check out of the hotel and take a taxi a mile through a maze of busy streets to a market district called Huascar. My plan is to catch a ride in an open cargo truck to a distant town called Ocangate where I will begin my month-long trek in the mountains, making portraits of both the landscape and the native Indians. My taxi driver warns me to watch my bags with my life, as the market is notorious for its thieves. I assure him that I will be cautious.

In the busy marketplace, I sit with my back against a brick wall, my legs purposefully touching one of the two gigantic rucksacks resting on the pavement. Within two minutes, the larger of my two rucksacks containing all my camping gear is plucked into thin air. My eyes had been diverted for five seconds, off watching the sun as it outlined a cloud in the distance.

It is, of course, devastating. My mind gropes for the meaning to the simple unadorned fact that eight hundred dollars of goods that I desperately need are no longer part of me. On the black market, the bag's contents will fetch enough money for the thief to live comfortably for five years. No soul searching on his part will overrule the fact that he is free from hard toil for many years.

The world changes 180 degrees from benevolence to malevolence. I hate every person who comes under the quick scrutiny of my eyes. They are all capable of the act, yet each continues weighing fruit or lashing sacks together as if they are oblivious to what has just happened.

I try to take a few minutes to slow down my breathing, to intuit what indeed is going on from a higher standpoint than my apparently desperate mind being attached to my material possessions. I try to humor myself, calling up my best black comedy to carry me out of this hellhole of anger and disbelief. The internal dialogue goes something like this: "Okay Ethan, you've just had everything but your camera bag and a few personal items stolen and you are freaking out. You mean to say that you are upset about some scuzzy old sleeping bag and tent and bashed up pots and pans? Where has all your spiritual teaching and reading brought you if you cannot let a few possessions slip out of your life? What are you going to do when Father Death comes to steal the Big Baggage?" This little interlude has a two-minute calming effect upon my anguished mind, and then the frantic anxiety returns full force.

My introduction to South American justice, or the lack of it, is masqueraded to me by what God surely must have chosen from Central Casting as quintessential, crooked cops. Walking into the dingy police station at the bottom of the hill, six ugly henchmen stand smoking in a circle. Three are fat, three are skinny, all are seedy looking and wear deceit and mockery on their ugly faces. These men, I think, will most probably track down my thief, get the goods, and sell the items for profit.

One policeman with a fat belly and mirrored sunglasses returns with me to the scene of the crime and sheepishly asks two merchants some vague questions. Finally he shrugs his shoulders and walks away without so much as a goodbye.

I wander through the crowded streets, sick at heart. In the main plaza I am attracted to a tall man with long blond hair who reminds me of a Californian surfer. Approaching him, I ask if there is a chance he has camping equipment to sell. He smiles and says in a very American voice that his gear has been stolen, a few days earlier on the Inca Trail. After sharing my dilemma with him, we both laugh a little.

Nearing thirty and wearing an Indian poncho, sandals, and a red headband, Miguel tells me that he is a "channeler." I am familiar with channeling, a New Age profession where information from other realms and dimensions is revealed to people on this human plane by beings outside our own daily cognitive realm. I have read many books by channelers and believe that only higher, more advanced forms of life could have written them. At the same time I often feel that we are the channels for our own selves, that this higher information which we desperately seek comes from our own inner selves. I tell Miguel how during a two-year period I had regularly gone to someone in Vermont who channeled for an entity called Otawa. Miguel suggests that we do a channeling in his hotel room to find out why my bag has been stolen and what I am supposed to do now. I do not resist.

In his room at the Marquesis Hotel, a beautiful colonial residence from the 1600s now operating as a hostel for travelers, Miguel speaks in an odd resonant voice. The voice tells me that in a past life, around 1638, I lived here in Cuzco, near the market where my bag was stolen. I was a male Indian who farmed a hillside above the plaza, and a Spaniard with little or no power or influence had despised me for my physical strength and happy family relations. The person who stole my bag in the market today was that Spaniard, or at least his reincarnation.

The voice has information very similar to what Otawa told me a year or two earlier in Vermont: that I am a photographer traveling in the world, making portraits of other people's faces in a blind and unconscious effort at finding my own face; and that my photographs rest or reside in a type of depository in the sky called a *bardo*, where spirit beings with whom the voice is aligned are very proud of the images because of their humanness. It is the hope of these spirit beings that I abandon my proposed trek around Ausangate and cooperate with them in creating a book about the Sacred Valley of the Incas.

I am told by the voice to make preparations for an extended stay in the Valle Sagrado, what the Incas called the Sacred Valley, a one-hundred-mile-long corridor that runs from above Pisac to Machu Picchu, not far from Cuzco itself. Sleeping bag, tent, and guides will find their way to me. Most importantly, I will find many things for which I am consciously and unconsciously looking. I need only look for the town along the Urubamba River that will be expecting me. Precisely what town is not revealed by the voice, even after I implore it two times.

That evening at the Wisfala Café, I scan the faces, wondering who will tell me which town in the Sacred Valley is to be my home. Suddenly, goose bumps rise on my arms, the hair stands up on the back of my neck. A handsome Latino, dressed in a natty tweed sportscoat and tailored slacks with soft brown leather shoes, stands at the bar, leaning up against the mahogany counter. His jet black hair is wet and slicked down like Rudolph Valentino's or maybe Bogart's, his eyes are soft and watery. He seems to be expecting me. His mouth has a slight smile, as though he is about to answer any question I ask. I am drawn to him like some charged magnet.

Roberto is a Guatemalan who has spent most of his fifty years in Central America, San Francisco, and Spain. For the past year he has lived exclusively in Cuzco, as a businessman, an artist, and as an avid student of shamanism, especially those vestiges of Incan wizardry that still exist in the surrounding hills. He speaks perfect English and I am mesmerized by both his current Peruvian adventures and his past escapades, especially those of his years in Central America where he had been locked up in prisons in Mexico and

Nicaragua for having been too close to the true teachings of Christ for the establishment (*Guardia Civil*) to tolerate. He asks me to come by his small house in San Blas when I have time; he lives on a hill overlooking Cuzco, not far from the main plaza. Magically, he introduces me to some American friends who have just completed their trek. They sell me fine camping equipment to replace my stolen goods. As I shake his hand to thank him, he offers me a piece of traveling advice: go to the Sacred Valley and live with the local people in a village called Ollantaytambo, beside the Urubamba River. There is a lovely, beatific smile on his warm brown face as he says this.

The ride from Cuzco to the Sacred Valley on the bus is alluring, almost sensual, like a new lover undressing in front of you for the very first time. The city's traffic jams, congestion, and littered outskirts give way to groves of eucalyptus and the high terrain of villages of mud and thatched houses. Campesinos working in the fields wave as we go by. I sit at the edge of my seat, and wonder why we sit on the edge of our seats only at the beginning of our experiences. Too soon the same road becomes tedious, too soon we think we know all there is to know about dogs and cats, our soup, our bed, the sunset, the stars. I long for a time in my life where all roads, all relationships, all rocks and skies and flowers remain miraculously intense, where like the first drive into the mountains of Peru, I can experience the miracle of just being alive.

The bus is filled with mestizos, people of mixed blood, half Spanish and half Indian. The bus speeds through the *altiplano*, a high, windswept mountain plateau where llamas graze and small children, some barely four years old, herd large flocks of sheep and goats. Women in clutches of twos and threes stand with their backs to the whipping winds, talking, spinning raw wool on drop spindles into skeins of yarn. Somewhere before the ancient town of

Pisac, the bus screeches to a halt in front of a cluster of poor-looking, thatched adobe homes. The door opens and an Indian boards the bus.

It is my first real encounter with a South American Indian. I try and blot him up like litmus paper, straining with my nose to smell him, listening with keenness to his sucking on a wad of coca leaves that he has balled up in his cheek. As much as anything, I rivet my stare upon his redness, not his skin, for it is a delicate, cuprous brown, but his handwoven poncho, hat, and pants. Like a vermilion hummingbird he has alighted beside me. By his red dress alone he seems to be saying, "I am Indian, I was here first." Somewhere in my early teenage years I promised myself to become acquainted with Native Americans. I have learned to screw up my courage and engage them in conversation, asking them what people they belong to, and listening to the poetry of tribal sounds that fall from their lips.

Where the Indian gets off the bus—Pisac—is where the Sacred Valley begins. Here the mighty Urubamba River flows north toward Machu Picchu and its eventual confluence with the Amazon. Here in Pisac the smooth tarmac road stretches nearly fifty miles to my destination of Ollantaytambo. Geographically we are in another climate from Cuzco, having descended in one hour nearly 4,000 feet to an elevation of 8,000 feet above sea level. Here fruit trees grow in profusion along the river banks, and the fertile fields support large tracts of corn and other vegetables. A man in the seat behind me, a city dweller of sixty with spectacles and short cropped hair, quietly and gently touches my shoulder with an arthritic old hand and begins to explain things in simple Spanish. Five hundred years ago, he says, the Quechua-speaking peoples

who inhabited this valley carried their Incan kings upon litters from the capital of Cuzco to vacation in the warmer, gentler climate of this valley. Incan runners, called *chasquis*, used to run the Incan roads from the seacoast to Cuzco in only three days, carrying fresh fish and other delicacies for the Incan kings. *Chasquis* could run in relays between Quito, Ecuador, and Cuzco, Peru, a distance of 1,250 miles, in five days, and this at altitudes of between 6,000 and 17,000 feet.

The valley had played a key role in the development of the Incan empire. Its warm climate and rich soil were rarities for these high Andes. The jungle, which lay close by on the western flanks of the mountains, provided easy access to fruits and other plants which the nobles and the Inca himself undoubtedly enjoyed. Still, the Sacred Valley was probably no more sacred to the Incan people than any other parcel of land in Tahuantinsuyo (the four corners of their world), for everything under the sun, especially Mother Earth, was honored and revered.

On both sides of the highway, men and women work teams of oxen on the flat expanses of the river bottom, rich, dark soil churned up anew by the sharp-pointed wooden plows. Our bus stops in a small town called Urubamba, a marketplace center whose main square holds a pisonay tree with a girth so immense I judge twenty children can encircle it with their outstretched arms. Everyone gets up and squeezes through the bus door. A farmer hauling sacks of cabbages and chickens through the crowded door explains to me that we are switching from bus to truck for the remaining eleven miles to Ollantaytambo.

I follow the crowd of campesinos toward a waiting red pickup truck and take my place with some twenty-five others who are heading down the valley. Gear is stowed, money paid out (nine

cents), and we are under way. My fellow travelers seem even-tempered and smile at each other, speak Quechua to me which I clearly do not understand, and then laugh to themselves about the happy gringo who likes to ride with his face to the wind. A fat, middle-aged campesino woman with two gold front teeth hands me a topsy-turvy cup of spilling *chicha* (a corn beer drink) from a flagon at her hip. I hold up the cup and salute the people around me and quaff the somewhat bitter-sweet brew, half of it flowing down my shirt on a bumpy corner. Everyone laughs.

A gradual hill winds past giant pillars of Incan design and an aquamarine-colored shrine of Mother Mary in cement and stone. The gold-toothed woman pokes me in the ribs lightly and says, "Ollantaytambo." We pass slowly into the welcome shade of enormous trees, and past small Incan houses of stone where I can see a great many farm people and Indians. We are the only motorized vehicle to be seen in town.

For long moments I stand letting the sights and sounds flood into my senses. A sparkling-eyed, dark-haired girl comes up to me. I tell her I have just arrived and that I am looking for a place to stay. The girl, whose name I have trouble pronouncing—Eisabel (ay-ee-sá-bel)—takes me to a small pension run by a woman in her midtwenties named Pocha.

She comes to greet me, her small son on her back in a poncho like all the infants in Peru. This Pocha has integrity and warmth in her face; I sense that we will be good friends. She has a regalness about her, with long black hair finely combed and braided, a clean and pressed skirt, and smooth, clear skin. She explains that there are two rooms above her kitchen and both are vacant. The cost is a dollar a night. I take long minutes to absorb the view. Some ruins are near, two hundred yards down a cobbled street, then high up a small mountain of stone. Commanding the uppermost position is the Temple of the Sun, a stone shrine of six, standing granite blocks the size of school buses, each embedded in the ground and resting snuggly against each other. At lesser elevations are scores of monoliths, massive walls, ancient house foundations, and great terraces of stones. At the base of the ruins is a parking lot for tour buses. I choose the room with the easterly view, as Pocha says it catches the morning sun falling upon the ruins. The adjacent bathroom actually has a toilet seat and Pocha proudly shows me the shower and illustrates that if I want any warm water I will have to run the water at a desperately slow speed.

Eisabel waits for me on the lawn, inviting me to accompany her as she gathers fodder for her rabbits. Another girl, named Senovia, joins us on an ancient footpath that runs beside a turbulent stream. Often in my travels it is the first handful of new friends that remain

most special, not because they are necessarily the most personable, but simply because they are the first. Soon other children join us and we become a ragtag group of nearly fifteen. We climb stone walls, pass through meadows of wheat and corn, and eventually come to steep cliffs near the ruins at the edge of the mountains where the sweetest grasses grow.

The children begin cutting and gathering these grasses. So quick and dextrous and sure are they of the bitter-tasting weeds which their animals will reject that I sit in awe and watch as they forage a full quarter-acre. In their scavenging the children discover wild strawberries hidden deep within the grasses, some no bigger than a pea, and bring me three or four at a time, lingering by my side to await my smile as I taste their tangy sweetness. The children also bring me succulent plants that grow around the base of the stone cliffs, small minty leaves and lemon-tasting stalks that they want me to sample. They are bringing me gifts, small simple things, and I am deeply touched.

We hike up near a series of waterfalls where an ancient aqueduct brings down water from the mountain glaciers to the village cornfields. Eisabel and Senovia gather wild roses from prickly long vines that grow out of the clefts in the cliffs. They wear wreaths of wild flowers in their hair and with their white, gathering sacks tied about their shoulders they look radiant, innocent.

On our way home, we come upon tall, scarlet plants, six feet high and more, which the children seem to know, the bigger ones picking handfuls of the petals and smearing our cheeks with them, giving our faces an ocher-like color, an initiation of sorts for our

impromptu club. Eisabel begins singing a song about the Lord, to the tune of the "Battle Hymn of the Republic." "Gloria gloria aleluya, gloria gloria aleluya, El nombre es Dios [...His name is God]." The chorus of our ascending voices pierces the countryside as we amble home in the darkness.

I awaken once in the middle of the night. I have no idea where I am, and it requires ten or twenty seconds of mental groping to figure out. I lie motionless in the midnight hour trying to discover what country I am in, and whose bed this time, and even a sense of who I am. This has been happening for a number of years now, the result of being a traveler. Awakening from a deep sleep, I often lie and purposefully let the seconds roll by in which I am detached

from knowing who, what, when, where, and why. I am just breath, just present tense, just a mind upon some sheets and pillows. There is a minuscule strangulation in not knowing the answers to the most simple questions. There is a great deliciousness in not knowing, too. But then something within me wants all the pieces of the puzzle put back and I begin backtracking, feeling the lumpy mattress or listening to the drone of the icebox, telltale signs that bring me back into a conscious world. I am Ethan, I am in Peru, this is a village called Ollantaytambo, I am a photographer. And soon I know again. But somewhere in my mind I know that not knowing is even more spellbinding. Someday, I promise myself, I shall lie awake in non-knowing and stay there without trying to come back, for a minute longer, maybe more.

CHAPTER TWO

M Y NEW FRIENDS IN THE VILLAGE are Cristina and Alberto who own a bakery in their home at the edge of town. They bake round pita-bread that their children sell in the plaza at all hours of the day and night. Their four children, Mercedes and María, Armando and Jorge, wear the Ben and Jerry T-shirts I gave them. The bread-baking business is in their basement, where calves and sheep are often tethered next to the giant, earthen, wood-fired oven. I especially enjoy going there when the family bakes, for their kiln is typically Incan, a large, round oven made of bricks, stone, and sand. I have hot bread and butter every time I visit.

Cristina, Alberto, and I are the same age, give or take a few months, and we are forever joking as to which one is the *viejito*, the old one. They are good people, and they are a good source for local history. Alberto has been on the council for the upper Indian communities for years and knows the people and the landscape here. Cristina and Alberto also run a small store where a few household provisions can be bought. I go there at night after supper and buy warm bottles of beer and the three of us, set free from the day's activities, sit long hours at a dirty, rickety, red-lacquered table and talk about history.

Alberto and Cristina were both brought up in Ollantaytambo and raised on stories told to them by their parents and grandparents. They tell me Ollantaytambo is a very old village, a thousand years at least, maybe double or triple that, the very last of the Incan villages still to be inhabited in Peru. Other villages have only vestiges of Incan architecture, but Ollantaytambo's entire town plan remains exactly the way the Incas and the pre-Incas had built it.

Ollantaytambo's history is murky at best. To speak of its history from a scientific or academic perspective is nearly impossible as the Incas had no written language. Their knot-tying records called *quipus*, while certainly numerous in museum repositories today, mean nothing to historians without the long-deceased Incan interpreters.

Cristina and Alberto tell me that the village was probably built by an equally great civilization long before the Incas came on the scene, that the massive stone temples, storehouses, and residences were fashioned of stone by these early people, then reshaped or incorporated by the Incas. The town's name of Ollantaytambo, familiarly known as Ollanta (Oh-yán-ta), was derived from an

early local chieftain of that name who had a forbidden love for one of the daughters of his sovereign, the Inca, Pachacuti. A great battle had taken place here between the Spanish and the Incas which the Incas eventually lost, and the village was abandoned for many years by the local residents as they made a last-stand effort to defeat the Spanish at a mountain fortress called Vilcabamba. Alberto, who drinks many more warm beers than Cristina, slobbers his saliva as he emphatically retells the war stories of his Incan forebears, arms flailing and black beard shimmering in the candlelight. Cristina, demure and soft, kicks my leg under the old table and smiles as her husband presents the next installment of our history lesson.

Everyone in Ollanta is a farmer, if not by profession, then by sheer number of hours spent toiling in the fields. Whether one is a seamstress or a butcher or a baker, one is still a farmer and always connected with the family lands. One of the things I notice about these farming people is that they do not seem to look upon their work in the fields as drudgery. It is their life, this growing of food. They take time with it and seem to enjoy it. The resentment so often associated with work, usually in industrialized countries, is just not here, a rarity, I think, today when often work is just to pay for necessities. Early Spanish chroniclers wrote that the Incas intuitively combined relaxation and labor in one breath, not separating work from worship. It is refreshing to see grandparents as old as ninety, and children, some barely three, working alongside one another in the fields, sowing seeds for a future harvest.

During the day when the children are at school, I often work with the men and women in their family fields, called *chacras*. I enjoy walking behind the surging teams of oxen and dropping small, brown seed potatoes into the yeasty, damp soil. The villagers seem happy to have a gringo in their midst. Today I plant with Alberto and Cristina and their two young sons. The noon heat is oppressive at this dry wintertime of year; sweat pours down my face as I try and keep up with the boys. I am barefoot, as they are, and my skin is bruised and caked with earth from walking in the furrows. The small stones we clear are easy to gather, but the large boulders, pushed up from below by the shifting earth itself, demand group effort. Cristina and I thrust our full bodies against the girth of one boulder, and Alberto and the boys pull upon it with ropes until it is painstakingly manuevered to the field's edge. We fall exhausted upon the ground, our breathing labored and resonant in the thick noon heat. Alberto, laughing, says he is selling the oxen and will retain me as their beast of burden.

We break for lunch in the shade of a nearby eucalyptus grove. We sit Indian style with our feet straight out in front of us as we eat. Cristina has brought beans and bread, and spicy cold trout which Armondo and Jorge netted out of the Patacancha yesterday, a small tributary of the Urubamba that flows past Ollanta. A huge stoneware jug of cold *chicha* beer is passed around, the grownups gulping huge mouthfuls of the tart drink, becoming a little tipsy. At meal's end, lying about in the shade, I inquire about land ownership. Alberto launches into a profuse explanation.

Here in the Andes, he begins, people are having a hard time producing enough food to feed themselves. This has not always been so. It was much different back in Incan times, for they were great farmers and could stave off years of starvation and drought with elaborate systems of *ayllus*, or communities, as well as storehouses and granaries.

As Alberto speaks, he points with his worn hand to an ancient stone edifice on a nearby slope which he says served the Incas as a storehouse. The Inca's plan of agriculture endured until the Spanish came and destroyed the whole system. It wasn't until 1967 in a sweeping social reform that the land was returned to the people. But the hiatus of three hundred and fifty years may have been too long. Much has been forgotten about taking care of the land.

Cristina interrupts with a sad look upon her beautiful face. In certain years, she says, hunger has become so acute that peasants have been known to practice infanticide, while older children are sometimes sold off as servants to the rich in Lima suburbs. The going rate for a fourteen-year-old child can be as little as fifty sacks of corn. And now, because inheritance and marriage customs continually fragment and scatter a peasant's fields over numerous villages, the average peasant spends three-quarters of his time walking between fields that sometimes are not much bigger than a bedspread.

I ask my friends whether they remember any stories the old people had told them as children, about their ancient cousins, the Incas. Alberto smiles and tells me he has seen an ingenious piece of agricultural wizardry, not far from here, just over the next valley in Moray. It is an earthworks, neither city nor fortress nor ruins. Long ago the old people made an incredibly important discovery in Moray. There were deep natural bowls that caught sunlight and shade in such a way as to create large variations in temperature within a small area. In the ninety or so feet between the top and bottom levels of Moray's main earthwork depression, there is a full fifteen degrees difference in temperature. Nature created in Moray the conditions modern man creates in greenhouses. And the development of the agriculture followed step by step, particularly with maize, the one crop that enabled Andean man to settle in large communities. Over half of the world's foods were first

developed in the Andes, from papayas, peppers, tomatoes, avocados, chocolate, cashews, beans, and strawberries, to strains of corn, squash, and potatoes too numerous to count.

I am coming to know more and more people, thanks to Alberto and Cristina. My favorite new person is a medicine man by the name of Carbajal. He is a short man with twisted legs that do not work well, necessitating the use of handmade wooden crutches. Though his humor is delightful and the music he plays on his battered violin is charming, it is his sense of power over darkness that most enthralls me. In the weeks following our first meeting, we weld an enthusiastic friendship. He is an ally of mine when the dark shroud of South America's lack of an honest judicial system descends upon the village and every man, woman, and child feels vulnerable to being unjustly arrested at night. I rely on him to calm me down when the police in town peer at me with suspicion, as if I were a photo-journalist doing a muckraking story on the corrupt department, or when drunken men want me to join with them in their debauchery and card playing at all hours of the night, or even when the weather turns stormy and dark and appears to be making ready for a flood that will wipe us off the face of the earth. It is old Carbajal who allays my fears, with coca readings, old Inca songs that he sings to me, and even his old worn hands upon mine as I sit at the edge of his bed.

Carbajal is not pure Indian. He is a mestizo, half Indian blood, half white blood. Still, I believe that his magic is pure Incan. He has a wife and eleven children, most of them living in their two stone rooms by the train station. His wife, a woman with a hatchet face and a heart of gold, likes me; she feeds me whenever I come to visit the old man. And I come often, to have a coca-leaf reading or to bring packets of herbs and flowers and such to the spirits in the surrounding mountains that Carbajal names for me. Stumbling through their dooryard cluttered with pigs, chickens, cows, and sheep, I usually wait my turn in a line of fellow customers who seek out his advice. Sheepskins hang on the stone walls inside the kitchen area, and Carbajal sits on his timber-framed bed holding court to a great entourage of people all day and night. He is a very popular man in town and seems to fill the needs of the villagers in the realms of body and spirit, from healing to exorcism and clairvoyance.

I have also met a Spanish doctor, a woman, who has been living in Ollanta for the past three months. We meet in the market in town, our hands nearly touching as we sort through day-old carrots and beets in the bins. Her name is Rocío, which means "dew" in Spanish. With a pleasant, wild determination about her that is enlivening, she is a petite, single, lady doctor working alone in the mountain communities. She is a medical doctor in general practice, but accupuncture is her speciality. She confides that the needles have not gone over well with the Indians and the campesinos, who shy away from these unfamiliar doctoring tools. Still, she is currently inoculating infants and small children in the outlying districts against communicable diseases, at her own expense.

She stays in a small white cottage in a compound that belongs to Doña Eva, a matriarch of Ollanta. Doña Eva allows us to take tea and cookies in the dooryard, but night visiting is never permitted. Rocío is a good person to know here, one of the only people in town who speaks English. On warm winter afternoons, when the mountainsides of snow and ice are gold and pink in the waning sun, we sit and talk for hours, mostly about Ollanta and its customs and people. One of the ardent bits of advice she gives is for me not to be swept off my feet by the landscape's desperate beauty, nor made giddy by every villager's handshake and hello. It is just a town, she says, no better, no worse than other towns in Spain or America. It rains here, people can have sour faces, the men often beat their wives, people steal, and the meat is often rotten. Be willing, she advises me, to see the ordinariness of it too.

The altitude sickness common to travelers here has begun to affect me terribly, especially when I trek in the mountains above ten thousand feet. I often have headaches and nausea and depression, not exactly great things to have when I want to explore this amazing landscape. The locals call this sickness *soroche* and are quick to tell me that I should go local and start chewing the coca leaves. I am told that most everyone in Ollanta over the age of fourteen chews coca, as well as everyone in the Indian communities. Swallowing the thick green saliva from a bulky wad in one's cheek relieves thirst, hunger, cold and fatigue. "Relieves" is perhaps not the right word. Coca leaves, from which cocaine is derived, probably only postpones these symptoms.

My baking friends, Alberto and Cristina, have taken a keen interest in showing me how to chew the coca leaves. They instruct me how to recognize good leaves in the markets of Ollanta, small bags the size of grapefruits neatly housed in soft white cotton. They show me how to make a wad the size of a walnut in my cheek, with a pinch of lime that helps extract the psychotropic juices. When the liquid residue is swallowed, I sense a mildly hallucinogenic effect on my body and mind, my whole mouth falling asleep as if shot up with novocaine. I climb with renewed rigor, running along the trails like an Indian. The leaf contains an alkaloid that has entered medicine as cocaine. I am told that millions of people in South America use the plant on a daily basis.

Botanically known as *Erythroxylon coca*, it is cultivated on the warm slopes of the eastern Andes. It is a low, thick bush with glossy leaves not unlike tea leaves. The leaves are picked four different times during the year, carefully sun-dried and then carefully shade-dried to retain the green color. Alberto says that coca leaves were chewed by the Incas, though probably limited to the priests, nobles, and soothsayers for divination purposes. After the conquest by the Spanish, the colonists enlarged the cocaine trade and the church got richer from the laundered drug money. It was once widely used as a local anesthetic in Europe and parts of the Americas and up until 1900 was thought to be a wonderful nerve tonic. Sigmund Freud was an inveterate user.

This morning the glass door of my pension opens and three gringos enter cautiously, ducking their heads under the low doorway and scooting sideways so that their packs can allow them to enter. They are two tall men—Nordic, I think—and a similarly blond woman in her early twenties. We say hello to each other in Spanish, (*hola, hola*), their faces imperceptibly inquiring of mine whether the food is good here, and are there any vacant rooms. They must have just arrived, perhaps on the morning train from Machu Picchu. In Spanish I ask them which country they come from. Sweden, they reply. These are the first Swedish travelers I have seen this trip. Germans, French, Dutch, Brits, Aussies, Kiwi, and Yanks all beat them in sheer numbers. I like the Swedish travelers I have known. They are handsome people, a bit reserved, but even tempered and well mannered. I chide myself on categorizing travelers by the countries they come from. I limit my gossip to generalities. The Dutch are whimsical, the Germans resourceful, the Brits have an eccentric sense of humor, the Aussies are great drinking companions, and the Italians are handsome, handsome, handsome. But I like the Yanks from the States best for some reasons I have not fully sorted out yet.

Gringos pass through Ollanta like migrating birds, though their numbers are extremely small for such a romantic spot. At any given time in a population of nearly two thousand, there are not more than seven or eight gringos putting up at the three pensions. These are the traveling gringo-types, the ones with backpacks, dirty socks, and stringy hair, with dust in their eyes and wind-burned faces. They are a colorful lot, seeing the world on a shoe-string. They sleep under bridges and eat local food, they ride the cargo trucks through the long nights, and soak their weary bones in the first hot spring they come to. They have quit their jobs back home without the slightest assurance from their bosses that jobs will be waiting for them when they return. They live in the mo-ment, inhabiting a free-spirited world of tramp steamers and capuc-cino on terraces under full moons with a gaggle of fellow unwashed travelers from a dozen countries, the Tribe of Travelers.

Some stay a day or two in Ollanta, but never more than three. They are shocked when I tell them that I have been here for three weeks and plan to stay longer. "Don't you want to see the rest of the country?" they ask me. "No," I say, "I am very happy right here."

This morning the Swedes are moving on to Cuzco to meet up with four Germans who are coming in today from Bolivia. I ask them to join me for coffee and eggs. They put their packs in the corner where they can see them, then slowly come across the tiny room in their clodhopper mountain boots and ripped short-shorts. They are tan and long haired, and their eyes sparkle. The two young men are Lars and Nils, the young woman is Gretta. Pocha brings strong coffee and bread, and my companions ask for only a bowl and some milk for the granola they have retrieved from their traveling sack. Pocha does not flinch; over the last six years she must have seen many gringos of every description cooking or preparing at her very table, food they brought themselves.

Over breakfast we four talk about travel, where we have been, what is good and not so good. Travelers are always asking questions of one another, questions which become the catalyst for new trips in the future. Matted journals, grimy with age and abuse, are extricated like the clay tablets of Moses. Information is passed about. Like silk merchants describing bazaars and robbers' roosts along the trade routes, we pass along what we have written down or remembered.

Gringos are forever bumping into each other. It is not unlikely that the travelers you share a fleabag pension with in Paraguay will end up at an Indian market in Peru six months later. By word of mouth over the years, a network of great places has been built in Mexico, Central America, and South America. Commonly called the Gringo Trail, it is a magnetic route taken in logical and illogical sequence spurred on by hearsay and travel books. In some ways it is like traveling in Europe or Down Under in that you get to meet hundreds of young and old foreigners, sharing cold showers, hot springs, and thirty-cent rides through long, cold, rain-filled nights in the backs of trucks. Addresses are exchanged, and promises to write are made, especially if there is a chance you will get to the other's country some time next year. When you see each other again, be it in Cuzco or London, you share hugs, kisses, smiles, and lots of new travel talk.

There are tourists, too, in Ollanta. Great numbers of buses come to view the ruins and the last of the still-inhabited Incan villages.

Sometimes as many as twenty buses drive past my door to the base of the ruins. These tour groups keep distant from the ordinary people of South America. I watch them as they enter Doña Eva's little store and stand timidly in line to buy a soft drink. They tiptoe in as if the people on the blackened earth floor of spilled kerosene and grease will eat them, or sacrifice them to the old Incan gods. The locals continue to look eagerly at them even after years without interaction; I think they want to talk to these white people. They are appreciative, of course, of the little money that they spend on soft drinks and handicrafts. But somehow I sense that the local people want the tourists to unbend and loosen up, get down and slap 'em five, laugh some, treat an old man in the corner to a free beer. The back streets go unvisited, the food is rarely taken in the cafes, and a one-to-one experience between someone from Belgium and someone from Peru is missed, time after time. They will go home on the buses, hand out the empty Coke bottles to the children's outstretched hands, and wave farewell like Queen Elizabeth to a village they never got to know.

I spend time every night in the plaza, playing with the children or visiting with the women and their babies as they wait for the heavy cargo trucks to roll through on their way northwest to the jungle city of Quillabamba. Night is when the eight or ten stores along the main street do a brisk business, the farm men gathering in groups by the kerosene barrels to talk, and women catching up on news as they stand in line to buy butter, sugar, and tea.

In the plaza there is a garden where the little children play a game of tag called *chapa chapa*. It is easily one of my favorite pastimes. There are three stone benches which serve as safety zones, otherwise all territory is no man's land and you had better watch out as the two or three who are "it" can tap you. Even though I have the longest legs of the twenty or so who play, the little ones are

lightning fast, evading my grasp in a split second by turning familiar corners and running around a tree. We all become very giddy
during these games and shriek and hoot, oblivious to the rest of
the world.

With the older kids, I bring out the blue frisbee. Amelia, eighteen,
is easily the best player of the group, able to send the blue disc
long, straight yards through the night air. There is something very
satisfying about playing this frisbee game, where words seem less
important and the communication is through a totally new form,
a flying disc that connects two people. It's simply in the flick of
the wrist, the spinning four-second trajectory, and the anticipation
from the thrower that the effort is good. Two inches from the
pavement, or with a leap into the sky, you grasp it. Got it. Thanks.
You're great. I love you.

The mothers who sell the food in the plaza at night range in age
from twenty to fifty. Most carry babies on their backs wrapped
in the striped, woolen ponchos. Some sell a sweet, mashed bean
punch that they keep warm over small fires of twigs inside tin
pails. Others sell street food consisting of tamales (pulverized corn
cooked in brown corn husks) or braised, skewered meat, perhaps
a creamy soup, or fried fish and rice. Their customers are not
people from Ollanta who can eat at home and save their hard
earned cash, but the travelers on the big cargo trucks coming and
going from Cuzco to Quillabamba, the jungle city eight hours to
the northwest. The women sit long, patient hours in the chilly
night air waiting for these trucks to come through, stopping as
they always do at the police checkpost in the plaza and giving the
passengers a twenty-minute layover. It is a busy scene when the
truck grinds to a halt in the plaza. The daughters of the women
stop playing *chapa chapa* and run over with their wicker baskets

of food to make a sale, their plaintive voices rising in the night. "*Plátanos, plátanos . . . .* " "*Choclo, choclo . . . .* " "*Cómprame, por favor, cómprame.*" (Buy from me, please, buy from me.)

The faces of the forty or so passengers on these huge cargo trucks fascinate me. They are from what the Incas called the Antisuyo, the unconquered Amazonian jungle to the east. It is a land of terrifying luxuriance with people of fierce, independent traditions. They farm a little but resist any form of organization and thus stay always on the fringe of society. Their faces remind me of the jungle dwellers from the Yucatan and southern Mexico, hatchet faces straight off an Aztec or Mayan glyph.

The trucks themselves are oddities for this rough terrain, too large for the narrow tortuous switchback roads, potholed and gullied from flash floods. Some are Volvos, others are Mitsubishis, others have no name on them at all. They are giants on the earth, eighteen gears and all guts, belching and choking their way through the mountains.

In the plaza at night I see the dichotomy of our lives. The children and I play joyously in the park and the large trucks roll through the cold night, passengers under blankets and tarps with wild eyes, like animals, peering out at us.

Often I sit with my back up against the smooth stone walls that line the plaza. An old woman sits on the stone bench shaving smooth the handle of her walking cane. A teenager rides slowly through town on a chestnut mare. He wears cut-off shorts and has no shoes, his legs are smooth and brown, and his face is calm and joyful. Four little girls play jacks on the stone sidewalk, barefoot, ragged skirts hoisted up around their dirty thighs. Three girls come to sit on my lap and we watch the world go by. The oldest, Maribel, ten, whispers "my lub" in my ear and we all laugh. Two old *viajitas* spin raw wool on drop spindles. Cows and bulls walk peacefully home through the old streets. Indians with supplies head up the Patacancha for their village of Huilloc.

The moon is up and discloses mists hanging on the two spires of Pinculluna, Mountain of the Flutes. Small boys and girls, no older than four, haul about their tiny brothers and sisters on their backs in sagging ponchos. This time of day, when the form becomes a bit formless, is my favorite time. I feel ageless, colorless, birthless, deathless, countryless, at peace. By day's end when I finally pull myself away from the plaza to sleep, my body and spirit pulsate. I feel hot to the touch, radioactive with the day's encounters.

◆

CHAPTER THREE

M Y FIRST WEEKS ARE SPENT walking the trails that surround Ollantaytambo. One day I walk up a side valley beside the flowing Patacancha, a hike of three or four miles on a broad well-used mountain trail. The walls of these granite mountains are bathed in dreamy winter's light, pale yellow and wan upon the dry stalks of the corn and the eucalyptus leaves that lie like a carpet on the trail. Campesinos come down from the mountain fields with their small bands of cattle, sheep, and goats, and old Indian

teamsters with long, wooden plows resting upon their broad shoulders drive oxen and steers before them. Woodcutters in ragged homespun leggings descend the trail with their burros and small horses laden with split, green wood oozing sap at the cut ends. There are school children in their gray uniforms and with scrubbed faces en route to school, and there are also many other children too young or too poor to go to school, whose job it is to herd sheep and goats on the high chaparal during the day. All these people, from young to old, from campesino to Indian, greet me in some way or another, with a handshake or a smile, with a salutation in Spanish, or Castellano as it is called here in the mountains. Many speak the Quechua to me, "*Allinllachu?*" (How are you?) Or, "*Alabado.*" (Praise God.) I try to respond in Quechua, "*Allillanmi kasiani.*" (I am fine.)

Many travelers along the trail are Indians coming down from their surrounding communities, or *ayllus* as they are called in Quechua, to trade in town for kerosene, matches, tea, and oil. Others are returning on the trail with provisions in a cloth bag slung over their shoulders. With their short powerful legs they overtake and pass me easily, though some seem intent on walking a few hundred yards with me, trying to unearth who I am and from where I have come. One Indian man who looks like a wizened old Incan warlord in his skullcap and poncho, barefooted and bent over with an enormous load of cornstalks upon his back, hails me along the path and asks me a question in faltering Spanish, something about the train schedule and what time it is now. I answer as best as I can, taking time to look deeply into his face, to simply absorb as much as possible of him in the lingering seconds along the trail. He is a short, stocky man, not much taller than five feet, but with a massive barrel-chested torso and short, powerful, bare legs. I glance down once or twice to marvel at his callused and blackened feet, toenails clipped like some workhorse's in the forest. There is a faint aroma of wood smoke and grease about him; his cropped hair is jet black and glistens in the sunlight.

Farther up the trail, on a small plateau that neighborhood children tell me is called Manuepata, I pass a small, thatched house close to the stream where a celebration of some kind is in progress. Some thirty villagers, campesinos, not Indians, are eating and drinking in small groups; there is the sound of flute and harp music. A small child of three or four sits upon a table in the courtyard with several grownups cutting her hair. Two or three of the adults seem particularly animated and motion for me to join them. I descend a muddy trail, slipping as I go, and make an awkward entrance into the packed-earth courtyard.

The celebration is a ritual for small children called a *corte de pelo*, literally a cutting of the hair, usually for the first time. Sometimes a baptism at the local church follows, so I am told, but today there will only be the cutting and a small feast. The child upon the kitchen table in the courtyard, whose locks fall today, is named Felicitas. She is three years old and sits with a look of dejection upon her face. Her shoulders are slumped; she longs to be with other children playing in the fields. Alongside her crossed legs and frilly, white party dress sits an enamel pan with snippets of her black hair; crumpled ten *inti* notes (less than twenty-five cents) are piled there among the hair cuttings. The shears are handed to me by the girl's mother, a handsome woman of thirty with long braids and a full, pink skirt. I pull out some bills and lay them in the pan, then commence to cut a few of the still-long wisps about the child's neck. Little Felicitas looks up with true suspicion; I am sure I am the very first gringo she has ever been close to in all of her three years.

Chicha is dispensed, the giant harp and some drumming and a *quena* flute blend together to make memorable but not melodic music. Old men and women dance together, the men holding white hankerchiefs or white paper napkins between their fingers. Little Felicitas looks on with dismay. By now her hair has been cropped close to her head. A woman in her early twenties asks if I would like to dance. Her hands take mine with softness and warmth, her eyes assure me that she will show me the steps, and by now it is too late. The dancing is simple, a child could do the steps, and I am a little drunk from the three glasses of *chicha*. The world takes on a form and ambience that seems just right. How marvelous. I am happy.

After the dancing, I am escorted through the tiny doorway to be seated with honor by the smoky fire upon a sheepskin. The house is dimly lit by candles and the light from the smoke hole high above. When my eyes become accustomed to the duskiness, I see two old grannies seated across the way on the earthen floor drinking *chicha* and eating what appears to be cooked rats. Already my mind is formulating the words for a prayer to the angels above. Dear Lord, spare me, spare me from what I think they are going to serve me. As the final prayer word is said, one of the old grannies gets up and prepares me a plate of cooked rodent, grinning toothlessly as she places the plate on my lap.

I look down at the little critter and almost gag as I discern in the brown light its head and teeth and beady little eyes that seem to be looking at me. Even the long, curled tail and the shiny toenails are perfectly in place, though a bit curled up from the heat of the frying pan. What can it possibly be? I feel some creepy-crawly things at my feet. I bend down and see guinea pigs scurrying about, big, brown ones and pinto ones like miniature horses, and nasty little black ones that squeal as they sniff my bare ankles. Old grannie stands precariously close to me awaiting my first bite. The meat is gamey and oily—very rich—but not much different than the squirrel I have eaten in an Appalachian hunter's cabin, or bear meat, or raccoon. Still, when the old woman turns to shuffle back to her seat, I slip the carcass from my plate onto the plate of a small child beside me. She seems delighted to have ceremonial meat bestowed upon her, something that children probably do not get often.

I take my leave of the celebration as the setting sun illuminates the faces of the villagers. They have made me welcome in their midst today, on my first foray into the mountains. I kiss little Felicitas on the cheek. She is now up and about playing, and has apparently forgotten the harsh ordeal of losing her hair. I shake hands with everyone and promise my hosts that I will return another day.

It darkens quickly on the way home, light turning from orange to orange-black to blue-black as I follow the trail down to Ollanta. These winter days in the mountains are of short duration, more pronounced because of the great jagged peaks that block out the sky. I gaze up at the first few stars. The available sky is like some punched-out hole, small and narrow. How mysterious this mountain light, the dark ushered down through this narrow chasm of uplifted volcanic rock, light made more intense by its directed path. The rushing waters of the Patacancha whisper its evening song, some lone bird in its bower shrills the note of a flute.

Another sunny morning, Pocha encourages me to visit a mountain community of Indians and describes in her slow, sing-songy Spanish how her old father, Enrico Gutieres, had often told her of the small isolated village as a child. The village lies down river, then straight up into the skies on winding trails.

I hike down the valley almost six miles, past a village of ten houses they call Pihri. Five old men seated in a circle shelling corn tell me what I wish to know, the mountain path to the isolated Indian community they call Pucruyuc. These farmers are happy to be diverted from their labor to draw me elaborate maps in the dusty earth with stubby fingers.

Slowly I climb, for it is hot this day, the winter sun parching my throat and burning the skin on my nose and forehead, the pack like pig iron upon my back, my lungs bursting with the absence of oxygen in rarefied air. Near two small houses in some crenelated rock country, a huge mastiff dog comes running at me snarling. Two teenage girls, handsome in their work of holding back the brute, point quickly to the trail. I am gone fast.

Higher and higher I climb, four hours and more of laborious work on the narrow, switchback trail. All day I see no one, only the manure of sheep and goats. Twice while resting in the shade of scrub chaparral, angular cattle poke their heads close to me to sniff, then bolt. And when I doubt that this Pucruyuc even exists, I come within sight of terraces of black earth for potatoes and rude fences of logs which tell me the village is near. Another half hour's climb brings me to a pampa, or plain, not much bigger than two football fields, where six stone and thatched houses sit quietly in the shadow of massive mountain walls and glaciers. Surely I must be at close to 13,000 feet.

I approach a small house, call out in Quechua a greeting. The door creaks open and an Indian woman's head emerges. She is afraid of me, for I suspect I am the first visitor in a long time. Do I want to kill her, steal her babies, burn her house and rob them of their harvest? She speaks no Spanish and demurely points with sorrowful eyes to a man several hundred yards away who is watching his herd of llamas and alpacas from atop a high cliff. I look off to the man, silhouetted against blue sky and white mountains, and wave. He waves back at me, then bounds off the precipice and comes on the run. When he reaches me he smiles and holds out his worn hand for me to shake. His name is Tomás.

Tomás speaks elementary Spanish, enough so that we can under-stand each other. He is thirty years old. He wears the traditional everyday, red, wool poncho and handwoven breechcloth pants of his people. Upon his feet are cheap, rubber sandals. His bare legs are strong, muscular, and well shaped. His close-cropped hair hides beneath a broad-brimmed hat. We sit upon the grass and talk in the noontime sun. Pucruyuc, he says, has but the six houses that circle the pampa. The fifteen people who live here are all related.

Twice a month someone from the village makes the long hike down the mountain trail to Ollanta for supplies.

When I ask him if many gringos come to Pucruyuc, he laughs and tells me that as far as he knows no one else has ever come. I am the first visitor. Does this make me eligible for the so-called rolling out of the red carpet? He laughs again and then runs to his medieval barnyard and returns with a plate of still-warm potatoes. Together we sit and eat and share talk about his village and these mountains he has known all his life.

Hours later, I return down the mountain trail to Pihri, past the farmers who cheer and wave as I cut across some cornfields and head toward Ollanta. On the way I come upon two teenagers I know, brothers, with whom I have played soccer in town on a number of occasions. The leaves are going to duff on the trees, and the air is soft with breezes from the mountain's snowfields.

We pass by small settlements of three or four houses and peer into the barnyards, catching glimpses of burros swishing their tails and resting at ease, and small, bare-bottomed children playing in the sand with a stick and some stones. Old grandfathers chop wood, teenage girls wash their hair in soapy basins with towels around their brown chests, and hoots and hollers from the highlands float down from small boys tending their flocks of sheep.

The two brothers and I become one, kicking stones along the dusty road, drunk on the amber sunshine. We eat apples and parched corn we get from an old man beside the road, and we sing all the way home, the songs becoming sillier and more feeble as we doggedly plod the last few miles to Ollanta.

One day Rocío and I take a train downriver forty miles to inoculate infants at a small Indian community in the mountains. In the early-morning sunshine we wait beside the tracks with fifty or so other travelers, eating bananas in the warm air and drinking cups of strong coffee bought from a vendor at the station. Hardly anyone moves, let alone speaks. The air is subdued and zephyr-like, the brown waters of the Urubamba sweep quickly down to the sea. Finally the piercing scream of the train's whistle shakes us from our dreaming and with it comes a frantic, chaotic dash to board the oncoming orange and red coaches, even before they have stopped. Our train barrels into the station with Peruvians covering the outside of the cars' entrances and exits like flies. People hang out the windows, bending down to help friends pull up bags of heavy produce, while villagers from the ground shove sackfuls of produce into the already impassable doorways.

Rocío tells me in an anxious voice that we have only two or three minutes to board, no more than that, and that we have to push and shove, too, if we want to get aboard. We get behind a huge Indian woman with an enormous load of cabbages clutched to her bosom and allow her to block for us, slipping in behind her, only to find the interior totally congested, a madhouse of humanity. Every seat is taken, the aisles are jammed, and people have even occupied the coupling area between the cars, a frightfully dangerous perch. The whistle blows three times, the cars bump and jerk forward, and I find myself squeezed between some campesinos and a chewing gum (*chicle*) salesman with a mean face. Downriver we roll.

From the very start I find the train ride nearly unbearable. I have ridden local trains in India and Sri Lanka, but this one is far more demonic. The whole train smells of urine, as the bathroom doors are off their hinges (someone obviously had once needed some hinges for his house and had taken them). People relieve themselves without using water to flush the toilet. There are drunk men and women on board this morning, arguing. No one really seems to take an interest in their quarrels. One man eventually consumes one drop too much of alcohol and falls through the throng to the floor, vomiting as he does so on himself and those around him.

The train stops at small communities along the way and women with their babies who wish to exit with their bags of heavy produce panic and claw their way through an unyielding crowd toward doors that never seem to open. If these women do not get out, they are forced to ride another two or three miles and try and exit at the next station, then walk back home. There is fear and anxiety in the air, something that fills the train with a sinister, concentration-camp atmosphere. We are all prisoners of a system that does not work, a railroad as corrupt and broken as the rickety rails upon which it rides.

The mean-looking *chicle* salesman squeezes close to my chest and eyes the camera bag I clutch. Rocío whispers in my ear to guard my bag with my life; the gum salesman is a thief who is about to steal my cameras. I glower at the man, conjuring up from within me the worst possible face I can muster, eyes that tell him that he better not or I will get him good. Somehow my tenacious clutching of the bag and my stares hold him off until we reach Kilometer 88 and barely manage to squeeze out.

The train speeds away and leaves us in the warm sunshine. It feels like heaven to be off that monster, to have my feet planted firmly on sweet mother earth again, to release my tight grasp on my worldly goods. Still, I feel sad that these people have the single choice of riding the railed nightmare the rest of their lives or wearing out their sandals hauling their produce upon their backs.

The vaccination of infants this morning goes well, shy mothers appearing out of the hills with six-month-old babies inside their ponchos who bawl like baby bulls as the white woman pricks their brown flesh with the needles. I can see that the mothers are going away with a good feeling, knowing this time that one of their children stands a strong chance of surviving. Infant mortality in the Third World countries is high, especially so in Peru. In Guatemala, where I once spent two winters living in a Mayan village beside a lake in the jungle, my neighbors lost four of their eight children as babies from communicable diseases and bacterial infections caused mainly by the dirty drinking water from the lake. No one had ever told them that dirty water killed babies.

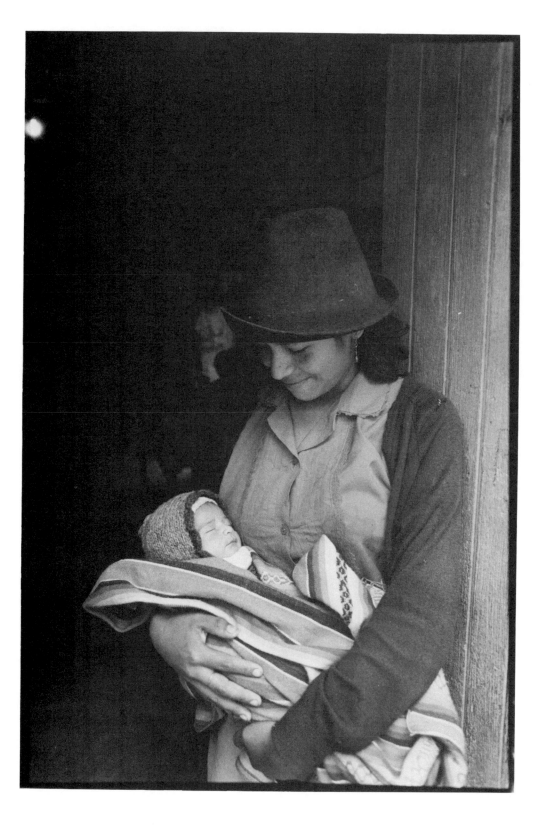

The ride back home to Ollanta is a carbon copy of the ride down, except instead of the sleezy *chicle* salesman there is a gang of Cuzco teenage boys a little way down the aisle from me. I know they have razor blades on them ready to slit with lightning speed my backpack, my shirt, or my pants to strip me of my goods. Often their tactic is to spill a foreign substance on their victims, like shampoo or mayonnaise or coffee, and while the person is worrying about the stain, the thieves slit open their gear and take what they want. Nothing like this happens on the way home, but when we reach Ollanta station I am exhausted from my constricted emotions, as well as from watching a sea of humanity go through their own anxieties and fears. Walking toward town, Rocío is able to lighten up before I do, explaining that robbery is an elementary part of South America, like the flu or taxes, but that it only occurs at certain times and certain places. I need not worry about Ollanta and the surrounding countryside. Trains, buses, markets, stations, these are the worst. But always, she says, take nothing for granted.

◆

CHAPTER FOUR

M Y CHANNELING FRIEND, Miguel, has arrived unexpect-edly from Cuzco on the morning mail truck, anxious to do a ceremony tomorrow morning at sunrise, at the Temple of the Sun on the cliffs above the village. These ruins at Ollanta were the very soul of the Indian communities that dotted this *altiplano*. Here, at the dawn of South American history long before the Incas had come upon the scene, some pre-Incan civilization, whose name and culture we still do not know, erected giant stones in the earth. Vast acres of stone terracing, sculpted stone baths, chiseled seats for the Incan kings, and labyrinths of passageways made of quarried stone served as their altar to the life-giving force of the sun.

How could any early civilization without the use of the wheel, metal tools, a written language, or draft animals larger than llamas have quarried these massive stones—twenty tons and more—from a far-distant mountain, then dragged them three miles down a mountainside and across a raging river, to eventually move them halfway up another mountainside? Whoever had built this altar left only the calling card of the six giant stones themselves.

I am only mildly interested in Miguel's suggestion, perhaps because I have read of late in books I trust that re-enacting ceremonies of the Native Americans can be disrespectful and dangerous. Besides, there is something about Miguel's strong personality that I find trying. I watch him as he violently throws his long, blond hair over his shoulders, as he accentuates a phrase, and this affectation disturbs my sense of what is humble behavior. He wears headbands and ponchos, dressing as if he knows something the ordinary person next to him does not know. Still, perhaps I only recognize all these things in him because they are painfully alive in me as well. I chide myself on seeing his faults and accept his kind invitation for the following morning, but as a spectator, not a participant.

The next morning Miguel and I climb silently the two hundred steps to the stone altar as the sun remains still hidden behind the needle-spired Pinculluna, Mountain of the Flutes. Like a bullfighter entering the ring, Miguel removes his brown, woolen poncho and carefully ties it about his waist, takes a handful of toreador steps toward the massive altar stones, and begins to dance. A faint ray of sunlight creeps from behind Pinculluna and falls at his feet. It is time to begin the ceremony.

Miguel places crystals, sacred seashells, and rocks upon a mammoth flat stone near the altar. He goes into a slight trance, imagining, I suspect, that he is an incarnate Incan wizard about to perform the ceremony that will surely bring luck to us as well as the sleeping village below. He lifts a clear crystal the size of his fist into the sky to catch refracted prism rainbows on his third eye, but is interrupted by a long, black shadow and a slow, deep voice. It is the ticket agent, complete with a ticket punch on a chain on his waist and a booklet of tickets in his hand. He approaches, not as an Incan farmer wishing to be annointed by the priest's ablutions, but rather as one who he is, the ticket taker.

Miguel tries to convince him that we are children of the sun and need no tickets. The man, who has a kindly face, tells us that we have to comply with ruin rules. Thinking now that precious time can be saved by hurriedly buying two cheap passes, Miguel whips out some money and throws it at the old man. But the gods are having a good laugh and the old man seems to have no change and thus goes into a long-winded but pleasant explanation about how one can buy a ticket good at all the ruins in the valley for a special price.

Miguel is unquestionably irked. He quickly puts away the crystals, seashells, and stones, sweeping them off the flat stone like some jacks player who has lost and heads home to sulk. He trudges back down the ruin steps, not like a proud warrior of the spirit would, but like a sulky child. I tell him the old man may have come as a special envoy, a messenger. Maybe he is an old Incan god. Maybe he is the Christ or the Buddha or even your great-grandmother. Miguel will have none of it and leaves in anger, taking the mail truck to Cuzco as I return to Pocha's pension.

Another day I hike the myriad trails that rise out of Ollanta, following shepherds, wood gatherers and Indians. Passing through the village or up along the high trails, I often come to partially opened doorways that lead to courtyards and barnyards. I am shy at poking my camera in—and do not—but steal sideways glances into their captivating interiors. Pack ponies with bleeding saddle sores stand hitched to a shade tree near sacks of manure ready to be placed on their backs to be taken to the fields as fertilizer. Smoke billows out of the thatched roofs. A granny spins wool from a clump she holds in her lap. Babies crawl in the black dirt, cats and dogs chase the geese, chickens, and roosters. Brown guinea pigs cluster at the entrance of the house. And a sow with ten little suckling piglets sleeps in the noonday sun.

Many times in my ramblings I am invited into the courtyards, often by school children whom I know, but sometimes by families I have never met before. If the sun is warm and the wind is down, they usually make room for me on a stone bench, the women of the house scurrying off to fetch a sheepskin for me to sit on. *Chicha* is offered if they have it (we gringos call it "the communion of the dirty cup") and sometimes a plate of still-warm, husked *choclo* corn, or a bowl of cherries or peaches.

These courtyards always seem neater, better organized, cleaner than their houses. I was somewhat shocked when I first saw the house interiors. They share it with their animals at night. A few of the village homes have wooden floors and are neat and tidy. But most houses in Ollanta and certainly out in the country have packed earthen floors, black from centuries of chicken droppings and baby urine and spilled kerosene and the blood of butchered rabbits brought inside to gut and dress. Hunks of horrible-looking meat hang from the rafters, where vast shoals of flies make their home. Most village houses have one bare lightbulb hanging from a roughly hewn rafter, while country homes are murky and dark with but one window in the roof to let some of the smoke out.

The doors on most homes are often just rude planks whacked together, the hinges made of uneven leather. Only a rickety table with uneven, handmade legs might grace the home as furniture. Everyone seems to sleep in one giant bed under mounds of dirty blankets.

I have never seen a book or a piece of art, except for wooden crosses or crosses made out of live cacti. Once I did see a woman bring in a lovely bouquet of cut flowers from along the road and arrange them in a bottle. But then she told me it was for the church and it disappeared out the door again, leaving the house very dark and gloomy and without simple, aesthetic charm.

One morning I awake with a feeling of great heaviness and depression. I turn over despairingly. I dread a down time right now, especially in South America, where dealing with it will take imagination and self-control, no girlfriend or movies or Red Sox baseball to serve as an antidote to this room full of blues. The village this Sunday morning is draped in winter gray, a pall is carried on a stiff, cold wind from the north. A few villagers struggle into the gale with their heads tucked down.

Rocío appears unexpectedly at my pension soon after breakfast as I clean camera lenses on the dining table. She, too, is feeling down. Over coffee we lament our situation. She offers a possible explanation, her belief that Ollanta is a very high place, full of light, but with a countervailing darkness which affects one's emotions in a schizophrenic way.

Outside the pension, the people look more ragged and dirty than usual, their houses in great disrepair, more stables than homes. The carcasses of meat hang in the doorways. Pig and dog shit seem to occupy every square inch of the cobblestone streets. I even catch myself thinking that the villagers are dim-witted. Rocío sees the same show, as if we have taken the same bad acid. How dismal and forlorn this South America can be.

Rocío, a devout Catholic, suggests that we go to the Church of Huanca, above Pisac, to pray. Huanca has been a very important place, for the faithful believe that Christ appeared there on several occasions some three hundred years ago. Each year near this time tens of thousands of pilgrims from many South American countries converge in the mountains at the church where they believe Christ supposedly appeared. I acquiesce. By 9:30 in the morning we are in the plaza ready to make the forty-five-mile trip upriver to pray at the church.

For nearly two hours we sit forlornly with our heads in our hands, waiting for a truck or van that never appears. Nearing noon, we get a lift with a melon man in his battered pickup as far as Pisac where we take a meal while waiting for a truck to Huanca, some ten miles to the south. If Ollanta looked dismal this morning, Pisac looks demonic, beyond the pale. The air is dull and the passage skyward to heaven seems blocked with dust and diesel fumes. Horns blare beside us, three drunks jostle our table with their stupefied bodies as they pass, spilling lukewarm coffee on our dirty plastic tablecloth. Coffee grounds swish around through the meat and rice I cannot eat.

Finally we get a ride in a small truck to San Salvador, a village at the very beginning of the Sacred Valley and from which pilgrims walk a half an hour along a mountain trail to a church under cliffs. Along the way we are menaced by four thieves, young men in their late teens, city youths, I think, who try to come as close as possible to steal our bags. I carry stones in my hands and occasionally let them fly. The thieves come close, but my stones ward them off. The huge church comes in sight and the thieves lose patience and head back down the mountain. They are warming up for the tens of thousands who will be coming next week for the Festival of Lord Huanca.

As we approach the huge church in a high *pampa*, Rocío's spirits begin to brighten. She seems animated and almost skips along the trail. I on the other hand can hardly breathe. My legs are rubbery and wasted, my head pounds. I am dizzy and spent. I drag myself to the church and grope my way along the nearly empty pews to Rocío, who is already at prayer. Truly, I have never felt so distant from my life. I have not felt this intensity of depression in the last ten years. This is not melancholy. This is death.

Rocío goes to the altar and I follow, past a diorama of life-sized wax figures of Lord Christ and angels as they appeared to the villagers some three hundred years ago. It looks as though Jesus has some kind of fire extinguisher upon His back, with angels hovering around Him. After a two-minute attempt at finding inspiration and peace in the diorama, I plummet back down the stairs to some vacant back pew and sink onto the cold stone floor. I want to surrender. But surrender to what and whom? To Christ? I have done so many times in my life but to no avail. I decide to surrender to surrender itself. I close my eyes and weep.

Rocío comes to me and asks if I would like to take God's Holy Mercy from the priest. I muddle my way to a small standing line. When my turn comes, I lamely hold the priest's soothing hand in mine and feel the shiny tassels of the holy sash annoint my forehead. He gives me the sacrament of the wafer. Immediately, the life force explodes into my body and my breath comes back and the headache goes away, and the nausea vanishes, and a strength returns to my bones. For the rest of the day things roll together with ease and benevolence. In my heart, I believe Jesus has spoken to me and I am deeply grateful.

At dusk, upon returning from Huanca, I walk up along a new trail toward alpine meadows that rise up like Mongolian steppes in the wan light. Passing a rude house of mud, with a straw roof and smoke pouring out through blackened thatch, I spy four school children playing "blind man's bluff" on the stony trail. I approach quietly and make a *silencio* with my raised finger to my lips. The girl with the cloth around her eyes continues to grope for the others in their play. I draw nearer and put myself in her path, she finding me, and reading me, as it were, with her hands. We have to bite our lips to keep from laughing, we four. Soon her mouth explodes in laughter as she blurts out the answer. "*Eres tú, Luis, eres tú.*" (I go by the name of Luis, as Ethan doesn't seem to compute.) She removes her blindfold, sees that it is true, and we

five hold each other and shriek and shriek and jump up and down with childish joy.

It rains in the night, and strong bolts of lightning and huge cracks of thunder explode overhead. I think the old Incan gods are hurling blocks of granite the size of battleships from off the mountain heights. The cobblestone streets bleed red-brown, a river of fast moving mud and debris. I watch from my window with my nose pressed up against the cold pane as villagers run from doorway to doorway with sheets of pink plastic over their heads and great arcs of water shooting out from their sandaled feet.

In the morning the sun comes out and the sky is blue and clear. I watch from my balcony as Pocha reaches up on tiptoes, picks a tulip-shaped red blossom from the flowering tree in the dooryard and hands it to her young son, Carlitos, to play with. Pocha, so beautiful in her skirt with her dark, straight, bare legs, moves into the kitchen to begin breakfast. I descend the stairs and take one of the tables that face out through the large plate-glass windows. It is my favorite seat, a place where the television set called Ollanta is never without a moving picture. Today it is young Alfredo, brother to little Sofia and older sister Abelina who often cooks with Pocha here. He is old enough to go to school but, for some reason I do not know, stays home with his huge woolly ram that pulls him about town. Alfredo peers through the window on tiptoes and his soft, almond-shaped eyes stare at me. He loves me, and grins. His ram, who always wears a purple sash about his neck, yanks him away, and only a hand waving goodbye can now be seen.

In the morning sun the Indians take time to wash off the caked mud on their feet in the rushing stream beside the pension. Other Indians throw down their cargo of new corn to wash in the fast-moving waters. The tourist buses have not arrived and the village

is still and quiet. Church bells sound in the gentle morning air, the tolling is rhythmic, like a blacksmith with a hammer pounding out an iron drum. Above on the mountain slopes, a few patches of mist linger. They swirl around the jagged peaks of Pinculluna and up around the Temple of the Moon.

A man with a slouched cowboy hat rides through town on a sorrel roan, its fuzzy, red colt on spindly, tall legs shying at cats and dogs and colorful scraps of paper. Two old mestizo men stand in the street and talk; they poke fingers gently upon each other's chest to bring home some point they are making to each other. Indians walk up from the train station and head up the Patacancha trail. A figure climbs steep, stone steps by a side street with an enormous bundle of corn stalks upon his back, trudging like a troll.

Everywhere women wash in the streams and canals, and teenage girls throw down their long tresses of hair and gently scrub them with soap, bending down on knees to wash the frothy lather from their heads.

In Ollanta, everyone lives within the sound of cascading water, be it the Patacancha stream, the Urubamba, or the myriad canals and irrigation ditches that course through the village. I am never out of earshot of tumbling glacial waters. At night I go to sleep with the soothing sounds of the stream outside my pension, a bare fifteen feet from my ears.

Sometimes after breakfast I slip through a hole in the ruin walls and walk to the ancient *Baños de Nustas*, the Baths of the Maidens, where I can be alone and still. Here the Incan maidens had once bathed in the natural springs. I lie on the soft grasses beside the stream and listen to the sound of cascading water as it dashes upon the smooth granite stones, falling asleep under the leafy branches

of a giant eucalyptus tree. Awaking, I open my eyes slowly, watching the snow peaks of La Veronica against the azure blue sky, and fleecy clouds racing past Incan ruins on the steep mountainsides. I go there to begin a day, or in the middle of a day to collect myself again, to be made whole by the running waters.

I carry my camera equipment with me wherever I go. I have doubted whether most of these country people would permit a stranger to point a camera at them, to capture their souls as some people persist in thinking. Here in Peru, I believe a man with a camera, especially a foreign man with faltering Spanish, is not always viewed with ease. Seven years ago sixteen photo-journalists were shot and killed as they entered a village for a look-see, mistaken by the campesinos for their enemy.

Somehow I am always made welcome in people's homes, and gladly given permission to make portraits. The people seem to trust me implicitly, and I am even sought out to come to their homes to make portraits. It is not uncommon for a small child to appear at my pension, knock timidly at the door and explain in a hushed voice that so-and-so is ill and could I make a family portrait while the person is still alive? Sometimes I travel on foot as far as ten miles. I do the best I can, coming on the run like a country doctor to make a special portrait. They love pictures of themselves and have so very few, sometimes none at all to remember a grandfather, nephew or mother.

I begin by photographing the children. They adore the attention heaped upon them. There are almost five hundred children in Ollanta, so that I am literally tripping over them at every turn in the streets. The are frightfully photogenic, almost totally unconcerned about how they look and more in tune with how they feel, which is usually buoyant and joyful.

The old people seem honored to pose. They believe that photographs of people should be formal, chests thrust outward and a serious, proud look upon their faces. They are so happy to have *fotos instantánea*, Polaroids, of which luckily I have brought a great supply. For children, and for that matter myself, the magic of watching a photograph appear on a piece of paper never becomes ordinary. I think I get as much satisfaction from the instant shots as do the country people, upon whose shelves and mantels the portraits proudly sit, complete with the names and dates inscribed on the back. It does not take long to intuit that everyone in Ollanta and the surrounding hills wants their picture taken—desperately. I am only too happy to oblige.

The first family I photograph is an old couple and their children who live way up the Patacancha in a typically thatched Incan house, over five hundred years old. Arriving at their home with my

rucksack of photography gear, two teenage sons usher me into the dooryard through massive stone walls and a large hand-hewn door that reminds me of entrances I've seen in Scotland. In fact, many of these Incan compounds remind me of the farming crofts on the Aran Islands in the Irish Sea, a landscape made familiar by Robert Flaherty's 1930s documentary film, *Man of Aran*. The seat of honor is given me by the hearth inside the house. The oldest daughter, a pretty woman in her mid-twenties named Impertisa, immediately goes about making me a meal on the smoky fire.

I lick the last morsel from my plate and watch the great flurry of activity as the family gets ready for their portraits. The father, Valentín Loysa Gonzáles, changes from his everyday attire of high-water pants of coarse, homespun wool into a natty, gray suit, complete with a matching satin vest. His wife, Alejandrina Espinoza, changes into a quite elaborate native costume of hand-embroidered shawl and skirt. When I position them outside with the grandmother in the dooryard, none smile, sensitive to the fact that they all have missing teeth. Instead, they thrust out their chests and stand tall, hands upon each other's shoulders. As I change lenses, Valentín scurries inside and gets the family's portable radio and asks if I will take their picture in the barnyard with their ox. The old and the new, juxtaposed. The two teenage boys, obviously from another generation and school of thought, pose in tight-fitting, white pants that they get their sister Impertisa to press with the old, coal-loaded iron. They have black, lace-up boots, and military-type, khaki shirts with meaningless epaulets on the shoulders. I try my best to get the boys to smile but they won't crack. Impertisa and her younger sister, Hermilinda, pose easily with their lambs on a stone bench in the back yard. This portrait session, and one hundred like it, occupy a good deal of my time in the Sacred Valley.

◆

CHAPTER FIVE

I RETURN TO CUZCO FOR SUPPLIES: GRANOLA FROM A SIKH RES-
taurant, peanut butter, petrol for my new stove, and some
photographic supplies. It is a chance to hear good music, eat
savory foods, and explore the city's ruins, especially up around
the famous fortress of Sacsayhuaman, or as the gringos affec-
tionately call it, Sexy Woman, an ancient Incan fortification
that reputedly had twenty thousand men working for fifty
years on its stone construction.

Cuzco is too interesting for me to stay away from, half Incan in
its origins, half Spanish, and now pleasantly seasoned with a smat-
tering of travelers from around the world. This was not always
the case. For centuries Cuzco languished in oblivion, outshone by
Lima and other Peruvian cities. But when Hiram Bingham from

Yale discovered Machu Picchu in 1911, the Lost City of the Incas, Cuzco was put back on the map. By the 1950s this "navel of the universe," as the Incas had called her, had become internationally known.

As I hoped, I bump into Roberto at the Wisfala Café and we talk about what I am experiencing in Ollantaytambo. "Keep at it," he encourages me, "and see where it is taking you." We also talk a bit about the history of his current home, Cuzco, though its origins are shrouded in mystery.

The Quechua-speaking people have their own myth of the city's creation. They tell how they came out of the lake called Titicaca on the present-day Bolivian border, wandered northward, and came to the valley of Cuzco where they laid the foundations for the great empire. The myth relates how the Sun God and the Moon God created the first Incas, Manco Capac, and his sister Mama Occllo, on the Isle of the Sun on Lake Titicaca. The Sun God told the brother and sister to teach the ideas of a great civilization to all the other Indian tribes. Manco Capac took a golden rod that sprang out of the lake and was instructed to stick the rod into the earth, and where it went in easily would be the site of the new order. The brother and sister wandered in true apostolic fashion for a long time, the golden rod bouncing out of the hard soil wherever they went. Finally in Cuzco the golden rod sank into the fertile soil.

Roberto says that archaeology has other things to say about Cuzco's beginnings. In 1941, an American archaeologist by the name of J. H. Rowe made discoveries there showing pre-Incan habitation, and some thirteen miles away at a site called Piquillacata stands a huge, pre-Incan ruin built by the Huari culture. Many cultures flourished in what is now Peru in pre-Incan times, Roberto con-

tinues: Chavín, Paracas, Mochicas, Tiahuanaco, and Chimú. Archaeologists in the past decade have excavated extensively in Peru, and while no written records exist, material evidence abounds. Unearthed is stunning evidence that monumental architecture, complex societies, and planned developments first appeared and flowered in the New World between 5,000 and 3,500 years ago—roughly the same period when the great pyramids were built in Egypt and the Sumerian city-states reached their zenith in Mesopotamia. The earliest sites are thousands of years older than their counterparts in Central America, traditionally regarded as the cradle of civilization in the Western Hemisphere.

"Quechua" or "*Keswa*" means "warm valley people" and indicates many things: a language, a tribe, a region. The Quechuas who eventually settled in the Cuzco Valley liquidated the earlier inhabitants, then began their polygamous society. These Quechuas, call them Incas, had the same tools and framework as all other civilizations: the polished stone axe, agriculture, irrigation, domesticated llamas, and the early earthcell commune called the *ayllu*. But what they obviously could do better than all their predecessors was to organize and systematize to such a high degree that they could tell the number of processed skeins of wool in all the myriad storehouses, down to the last fiber.

The early Spanish reported that Cuzco was like no other city they had ever seen. Certainly nothing in Spain could rival its treasured wealth. It was a city ablaze with gold, with buildings of huge proportions sheathed in gold. The Temple of the Sun and other buildings in Cuzco had been built of the most finely fitted stonework in the world. Unlike the Aztecs and the Mayas who adorned their temple exteriors with decorations and designs, the Incas preferred the simple sheathing of gold plate.

The most enthralling of Cuzco's edifices was the *Curi-Cancha*, the Golden Enclosure, where legends say that the first edifice had been erected by the first Incas. It had six major sanctuaries: sun, moon, stars, lightning, rainbow, and a sort of chamber house for the priests of the sun. The *Curi-Cancha* had a field of corn planted in gold and twenty llamas of gold and life-sized shepherds of gold. Even the roofs of these temples were reportedly laced with straw gold so that they shimmered in the sunlight. It must have been a truly magnificent city, its golden temples rivaling anything in the world. A handful of Spanish conquistadors stripped it down to its rock foundations in a matter of months.

We go to Roberto's small apartment in the San Blas section of the city, high on a hill overlooking the plaza and the plains of Huasao.

He is a most extraordinary person, this Roberto. He is so much outside the everyday world of nuts and bolts, though he does make his money these days from precisely that, building apartments on the outskirts of town. Still, he is only peripherally involved there with the architects and the engineers whom he blasphemes as idiots and offsprings of the almost insane South American way of doing business. He appears not to be interested in becoming rich with these building projects, nor in winning the approval of the rich Cuzco families by gaining prestige and power. He only builds them so that he can eat and buy art books and take a taxi instead of a bus.

It is his temperament, more than his astute mind and keen sense of humor or his comradeship or even his ability to help me along in this foreign place, that fascinates me. He seems unhuman, not in his unkindness, for he is kindness personified to the beggars, the homeless, the stray dogs, and the politically oppressed; he just seems untouched by ordinary human preoccupations with anger or possessiveness or greed or jealousy or repulsion. He seems not attached, at least not like most of us. I watch him as someone, a toothbrush salesman, knocks at his door and interrupts his afternoon nap by trying to have him buy a toothbrush. And this Roberto lets the guy come in, sit on his bed with his muddy shoes, even demonstrate how the brush works, all the while Roberto seems plugged in—or not plugged in.

Roberto's bookshelves are filled with books by Thomas Merton, John Lennon, Ram Dass, Rilke, Borges, Edgar Cayce, Gandhi. The white-washed walls of his bedroom look like a roadmap of Carlos Castaneda's mind, paintings he has done of the deserts where he often slept, and etchings of visions and dreams he has had. He writes poetry and drinks wine, smokes cigarettes, consumes coffee, and stays up late every night, reading or making love with Pili, his new young girlfriend from Lima.

Roberto is forty-nine. He tells me he drifted through Europe during the seventies, feet in both worlds of business and arts, with a dose of hallucinogens thrown in for good measure. Before that he had spent time in his homeland of Guatemala. He knows Nicaragua and El Salvador like the back of his hand. During the sixties he lived as a young artist in the Haight-Ashbury section of San Francisco.

Roberto's interest in Peru centers on his fascination with shamanism, the study and practice of using natural and supernatural powers to intuit and heal. He is always telling me about Indians and shamans. Roberto is particularly interested in the medicine men and women who are still practicing in the villages. As often as possible, he and his friend, Americo, a fifty-year-old University-of-Cuzco-trained anthropologist who speaks Quechua fluently, travel by jeep to the outlying villages to spend time with shamans, or *hampi-camayocs*, as they are called in Quechua. The most famous of these shaman healers is an eighty-five-year-old man living in a small village near Cuzco by the name of Benito. Even before meeting Roberto, I had heard of Benito, having read about him in one of Shirley MacLaine's books. Ms. MacLaine had needed the services of Benito in predicting when the rains would stop at Machu Picchu. Her film crew working on a television show was behind schedule as a result of unprecedented early rains, and she needed to know for sure on what date the rains would abate. Benito threw the coca leaves, prophesying that on a certain Tuesday between noon and two o'clock, the rains would stop. And they did. And the film crew was able to complete their work.

Rocío and Roberto are good friends, having met in Spain in the seventies and reunited in Cuzco and Ollanta this last year. They both know and love Benito. Rocío met Benito first at the hospital in Cuzco, where the flinty, old wizard was dying of pneumonia. Rocío, knowing that he would die unless something miraculous was done quickly, secretly performed acupuncture on him, and thus saved his life. From then on, Rocío, as well as Roberto, were welcome guests at Benito's house. Benito, when he comes into the city for errands, often spends the night with Roberto in San Blas, sleeping on a straw mat on the floor, as though he'd washed up on the beach. I am extremely interested in meeting him.

I stay the night with Roberto, and when Rocío appears in the morning we go by taxi the ten miles south to the fringe of the city and a small village called Huasao where Benito and his wife, Nate, live. Roberto shares with Rocío and me what he knows of shamans in Incan times. Everyone in preliterate South America, he says, had been bound to the wheel of the supernatural. Death, dying, crop failure, murder, shame, blame, these were the work of witches and bad spirits. Both medicine and magic were needed to exorcise the dark intrusion into human life. The illness of an Incan farmer mandated the calling in of the *hampi-camayoc* who might induce a fast or a salt enema, or perhaps herbals of roots and leaves. The remedy keeper, as he was known, had a superior knowledge of drugs and plants, some found only in the *selva*, or jungle, one hundred miles away. Quinine and cocaine were but two of the long list. But ultimately, despite massages, fasts, sweats, vomiting, and the like, it was the shaman's magic that brought the patient from sickness to wellness.

Huasao sits with a kind of quiet poverty under an open sky boiling with white cumulus clouds. There is a parched, windy look to the

town, with its neglected mud buildings in the shadow of gentle, rolling mountains. The taxi lets us off near the small store where a window full of delicate, brown faces look out at us. Turkey buzzards with long, ugly necks and sumptuous, black wings circle over ashen hills looking for the remains of feral cattle and other carrion.

The pathway from town coils past groups of men and women sprawled out on the ground, drunk. They call out to us as we pass with disparaging remarks and requests for money. "*Dáme plata, dáme plata, por favor.*" (Give me money, give me money, please.) Saliva runs down their chins, their eyes barely able to focus. One who speaks, an ugly-faced man, falls over backwards. The others, mostly women, grab his bottle and drink the remains. There is a sad and neglected feeling to this village, badlands of garbage and rubble where once the orderly *ayllu* granaries and school of the Incas had provided wisdom and bounty.

Benito's house is as crumpled as the rest of the houses in Huasao. He lives in a ratty, little compound full of chickens with almost no feathers and a rooster who runs after them all the time. Benito is sitting in the morning sunshine doing nothing but gazing off into the distance when we peek our heads through the wooden door half off its hinges. "*Pase adelante*" (come in), the old man says, failing to rise to greet us or do anything that breaks his communion with the sun's soft warmth on his arthritic hands and shoulders. Rocio goes to him immediately, bends down and kisses him. He looks up at her, then they hug. Roberto crosses the yard and bends down and shakes hands with the old man, and finally I, a bit shy and nervous, go across and greet him. At first glance, Benito looks like a simple campesino. Unless you look closely at his shining, other-worldly eyes that seem to shoot sparks into the

atmosphere, you think that he is like every other farmer who grows corn along the river and has a beat-up, old pickup truck.

Benito's customary gift to those who seek him out is to assist them in curing physical pains, or to read the coca leaves for divinatory purposes. We ask him if he can read the leaves for me. His wife Nate, an unusually small, spry sixty-year-old who speaks Spanish as well as her native Quechua, interprets our request and relays it on to Benito, who nods approval. With Nate serving as an apprentice and helper we proceed.

We all enter Benito's and Nate's small, dark kitchen. It is cool and holds smells of food, stale beer, and herbs that have possibly been burned as smudge-pot offerings to the spirits. Benito takes a long time to position himself on a poncho on the earthen floor. Rocio has brought her doctor's bag along and takes time to check the old man's blood pressure.

For a full hour Benito pours himself into the interpretation of the leaves that fall from his gnarled hands. He blesses the leaves, whispering to them through cupped hands, then holding them up to the sky and the four directions to ask for assistance from his *Apus*, or abiding mountain spirits. I hear him using the word, "Ausangate," on a number of occasions, the mountain I had long ago planned to encircle. Nate whispers to me that Ausangate is the source of Benito's power.

Nate, the sorcerer's apprentice, likewise fascinates me, for she seems half crazy, a little bitty thing with no shoes and a ripped skirt and blouse, playing the fool most of the time, head half-cocked like a chicken's, hands held close to her chest like a schoolgirl's. But when Benito requires her help in picking up the leaves from the floor, or making smudges to cleanse the leaves, Nate immediately becomes wise and intelligent, on par with her husband. (This is the way it is with those who have power, to remain disguised, underground, on the surface the fool.)

Benito tells me Ollanta is a good place for my work of making portraits and writing of the local people's ways. There is fertile ground for inner and outer changes in my being. When he finishes he puts away the leaves and becomes again a simple campesino, a Buddha-bellied, old farmer with black, callused feet who drinks beer from large bottles and laughs with us and eats hot, spicy chicken from an old, blackened pot near the coals of the fire. We toast one another and drink and soon depart. Four or five other groups are lined up in the old chickenyard on a log in the shade, waiting their turns.

On the way home in the taxi we are exuberant. I lightly touch my camera bag and tape recorder between us on the seat to make sure that the dream of recording the last of the Incan wizards is indeed true.

Apparently out of nowhere, Roberto flashes on the idea of starting a New Age health clinic in Ollanta, for the Indians and foreigners as well. His face is beaming, there is integrity and confidence in his eyes. "It wouldn't cost much," he says. We could all chip in. Benito and Nate could come for guest weekends. Rocío could do acupuncture. We could built a restaurant. What about making incense from the local flowers to sell? Pottery? We could get our friend Alfonso in Cuzco to train the gifted Indian kids to make the pottery of the Incas. We could even have Shirley MacLaine come down to do guest lectures. Music, photography, video, we could do it all. The half-hour ride back to Cuzco goes by in a

flash. A health clinic in beautiful Ollanta. We slap fives, hoot and holler, even go out to lunch and take voluminous notes. It's going to happen, and soon.

Roberto, Rocío, and I dine together tonight at the Wisfala Café. We make additional notes about the clinic in between bites of food. There is a new seriousness in our friendship, as if our real work has just begun, and we need to respond with professionalism.

Nearing dessert, two strange ladies enter the cafe and glide the half-dozen yards across the floor to our table. They are friends of Roberto's and greet him with the affection of mothers, kissing him on his forehead. Roberto introduces us to each other in a very formal manner. Doña Gregoria and Doña Catarina are tiny women with lazy eyes and hunched-up, petite shoulders and smooth-

skinned hands that they hold close to their chests as if they are brewing up some concoction. Roberto kicks me under the table and winks at me as he solemnly explains that Doña Gregoria, the swarthy one, and Doña Catarina, the fair one, are devout Christians who have a direct line to God. They talk to Him all the time.

Though these women cannot speak a single word of English, they seem to understand what we are talking about and launch into a sermon, half liturgy and half trance, something about what God has in store for me. They speak in hushed tones and take my hands in theirs, raising dark eyebrows to accentuate the importance of what they are telling me. The dark one, Gregoria, seems to be fully in a trance and knocks over my coffee with her elbow without noticing. I am becoming sensitive to the stares of the other gringos in the cafe. I pull my hands away from theirs, straighten up, and look at my watch. They look disappointed and hurt, but I am sure that I am not the first to have pulled away. They tell me they are coming to Ollanta tomorrow, as they feel it is an important spiritual center. Would I like to meet them? Roberto kicks me again under the table and I nod my head in acceptance. We will meet in the plaza tomorrow at 6:00 P.M.

The following day in Ollanta, the two little ladies appear mysteriously out of the woodwork, a half-hour late. The women are happy to find Rocío and me in the plaza and give us warm hugs and kisses. We four sit on a cold, stone bench and hold each other's hands, the night wind swirling bits of paper and trash around us. They are like little hobbit women, gnomes from some long-ago Christian catacombs unleashed in southern Peru. They immediately ask if we would join them in some Christian love songs. A cadre of teenage friends close by toss my frisbee; they want to engage me in some hip recreation. I cast them a resigned glance as if to say, sorry, guys, I've got to do this one.

The old women begin to sing and Rocío and I join with them in Spanish. The songs sound very sad, and while I cannot make out any of the lyrics except the name of Jesus, I get the impression they are songs of penance. It is a sad little scene, bent-over women in shawls in a now-fierce wind trying to evoke an ambiance for the Lord to change something in our lives. I would surely rather be throwing the frisbee with my friends. After twenty minutes of sorrowful singing the women abate. (I think the sisters of mercy are freezing and wish to seek the shelter of their own pension, El Tambo.) They implore me with all their heart that if I truly wish to see Jesus in the flesh (which I do), I must come to their room this evening and pray with them as they do at exactly midnight, not a minute before, as well as at three in the morning, and at six in the morning. I give my word that I will spend the night with them in prayer. Our plan is that Rocío will begin the evening prayers at ten and I will come a little before midnight.

At a late supper with Pocha in her tiny kitchen, she warns me to be careful with these women. She says that many foreigners are taken in by these kind of people. I tell her I will be careful, then go upstairs and pray by myself in my own room—to Jesus—that He might reveal Himself to me at the appointed hours. At half-past eleven, I walk slowly through the deserted back streets to El Tambo pension. Nearing the entrance, I come upon Rocío descending the stairs from the sisters' room. She tells me the two old ladies fell asleep early in the evening and that they are snoring away upstairs in their bed, dead to the world.

In the morning we look for the winged sisters of salvation but Raul Yabar, the crusty, old proprietor of the El Tambo, says that they have fled at dawn, gone somewhere to minister to the needs of the needy.

CHAPTER SIX

TELEVISION COMES TO OLLANTA ON THE evening of Friday the thirteenth, December 1987. Families, mostly store owners, wait like devotees of the Messiah for the exact moment when the wires from Cuzco are to be connected to the wires of Ollanta. Urubamba, the small city eleven miles up-river, has had television for nearly a year now. But this is the night for Ollanta. I turn from my game of tag with the small children to see the doorways of the little stores crammed with villagers, especially children, trying to get a glimpse of the tube.

The blue, hazy light from nine sets casts its pall over the plaza. No one wants to play *chapa chapa* with me. My teenage friends are over at their buddy's house watching the first television program. A teenage boy whom I have played soccer with on a number of occasions screams across to me, "Hey Luis, check this out. It's a dumb game show from Lima." I draw close to the crowded set and take a look. There, like some phantasmagoria, Peruvian contestants decked out in swim fins are trying to wind upon their twisting bodies some twenty feet of red ribbon. The kids are mesmerized; there is no way of breaking the spell. I walk unhappily back to my pension.

But strangely enough, the fascination with television does not last long. Something seems to bring the children back to the garden and their games and conversations with each other. The nine owners continue to keep their sets turned on at night, but people eating gristly meat and rice and beans with their coffee seem more interested in their food than in the idiot box. Still, it is here.

Roberto has come on the morning bus from Cuzco. I find him strolling in the warm sunshine, placid, handsome like a movie star in his white, linen trousers and white, Spanish-leather shoes, a pink shirt open at the neck, black hair slicked down. He takes off his sunglasses and gives me a warm hug. We enter my pension for coffee and Rocío soon joins us, Pocha taking extra time at our table away from the other gringos to make sure that we have everything we need.

Soon after, we depart through the glass door out into the morning sunshine to look for a spot for the medical clinic. Not far off, a few hundred yards toward the old church, Roberto halts by three old, colonial buildings, in bad disrepair, on a quarter-acre of green lawn. This, he says, is for sale; he has heard about it from his engineering friends in Cuzco. The price is right, but there are some South American complications, something about five brothers and six cousins owning it jointly. Roberto smiles and winks as I stare at him in hope. There is total confidence in his eyes. He is a master at unraveling this sort of bureaucratic, Latino redtape; he does it every day in Cuzco with building permits, bribes, wining and dining clients, simply being his wonderful, charming self. We can get it, he says, and we become jubilant, ecstatic, and grab each other's arms, smiling and laughing. It is the perfect site for the clinic, in town, protected by a police department in close proximity, with grand views of the Incan ruins.

I have gone into the mountains again, across the river and up onto the slopes of a place the locals call Cachicata, the Place of Stones, from where all the mammoth building blocks hereabouts have been quarried. Two teenage boys from the village are showing me the way. It is a three-hour hike along the river, then up into sheep pastures that eventually bring us to the base of the mountain cliffs. Here, a massive boneyard of gigantic, quarried blocks of granite, some weighing twenty tons and more, rest silently in the mountain stillness. The early sun worshipers in this valley quarried granite slabs from these dark cliffs and made a rampway of nearly two miles, down the mountainside and crossing the Urubamba, then another rampway that ran a thousand vertical feet to the site of the present ruins. I am having trouble carrying my own rucksack. How could they have moved such huge granite blocks?

The boys and I scamper over the remaining stones at the quarry. The Incan empire was laced with roads and temples, fortresses and cities, and towns nearly six times greater in size than those of the Middle Kingdom of Egypt. From Colombia to Chile the empire of the Incas stretched nearly three thousand miles. An irrigation system harnessed the water from the high glaciers to all their fields and homes. Rivers were straightened, sewers of quarried stone were fitted together, canals dug, so that everyone in the empire had the use of these conveniences. Terracing extended the amount of arable land so that even steep slopes could produce enough food for millions within the empire. It took less than two hundred years to accomplish these superhuman feats. Between 1200–1438 A.D., the Incan rulers expanded their realm beyond the narrow confines of their original valley to incorporate one hundred smaller nations.

Looking back down across the river and up to the Temple of the Sun on the distant slope above Ollanta, it is a difficult to comprehend how these early people, without the use of the wheel or large draft animals, and using basically stone implements, could have hewn and raised and transported such monstrous weights. Each stone was perfectly joined and the edges so chamfered as to merge without even a semblance of joining. A thousand years and a hundred earthquakes later, a knife blade still cannot fit between them. Many of the stone foundations of both temples and departmental buildings have joints with as many as twelve cut angles and have survived without a trace of cement. Who were these early people and where did they get knowledge of mathematics, astrology, architecture, and masonry?

On our way down from the quarry, the boys and I set up our tents near an abandoned farmhouse halfway down the mountain. We cook a dinner of *charqui* (dried-beef jerky, one of the only Quechua words to have come down to the English language) and corn over a fire of dried apple wood and watch the stars come out over the valley below. The mighty Urubamba, swollen from recent rains, hisses softly below us, and the huge altar stone of the ruins above Ollanta—once part of the cliffs above us—catches the last light of day. It is a fine clear evening, and the whole of the Milky Way splashes across the sky.

We lie with our rucksacks behind our heads and watch meteor showers in the east, dying embers of old stars coming to earth. Our voices become softer as the night's cold comes upon us; we stir the fire and draw our sleeping bags closer to our bodies. Twice during the night we rise to scan the sky for UFOs, the boys becoming excited about several circling satellites which arouse their curiosity. They eventually close their eyes and sleep, leaving me with the howling winds and a racing, small moon. A feral cow wanders past me in the night, then two mares, grotesquely

unfamiliar to me with their hobbled front legs impeding their gait. The boulders above me look down like sinister gargoyles and make my intermittent dreaming chaotic and ribald. I awake to a sun-filled morning with the whole world swimming in gold.

◆

I have just returned from the Christmas holidays in New England. Over the years I have found that no matter how enthralling the adventure travel becomes, there are within me certain needs, certain responsibilities that I honor. There's family to be seen, bills to be paid, work to be done on the farm with Marc and Sarah and their boys in Vermont where I live, buildings to be painted and cars to be repaired at my mom's in Connecticut, and to reassure Taylor, my son at Middlebury College, that I am there for him whether he needs me or not. This time I spent most of the holiday with old Harry, my beloved, adopted grandfather, sitting by his hospital bed and watching the grace and dignity of his dying.

I have brought gifts for my friends, and for Roberto, I have put together a whole trunk dedicated to him. Matted photographs from around the world will grace our new restaurant at the health clinic, along with books on how to make incense from wild flowers. I have a natural foods cookbook from the Horn of the Moon Cafe in Montpelier, Vermont, Leonard Cohen and Janis Joplin tapes, the *Tibetan Book of the Dead*, an extra camera for him to use, assorted knicknacks for his apartment, and considerable cash in a money pouch for the medical clinic. I have brought toys for my godchildren, Ben and Jerry T-shirts for teenage friends, and pins and needles for the old women. To Cristina, my baking friend, I have given an orange blouse. I bite my tongue to hold back the euphoria as she emerges from her kitchen having just donned it.

And for Alberto, her husband, I have brought a small kerosene stove. He is beside himself with joy, as he will be able to use it during busy times at his small store to make hot soups for his customers. Most of all, the villagers love receiving photographs that I have taken over the last few months.

On my first afternoon back in Ollanta, Eisabel passes me on the street with her friend, Senovia, and we laugh and hug. Soon other children come, their faces dirtier it seems than the last time I saw them. We wind our way up along the village streets, picking up an entourage of almost thirty kids. I pass out photographs; the children are frantic to see their own images, perhaps for the very first time in their life, recalling a day, an afternoon, a picnic, or a hike, a memory squirreled away in their small heads. With great shrieks of joy they explode when their name is called out. Others are stunned, like prisoners of war, not to hear their name called. Surely, their eyes plead, don't you remember the shots you took up by the waterfall? I wish I had printed every single shot, but I couldn't. A little girl named Kusi gets five photographs, puts them down her dirty sweater to savor later, and blinks stoically at me. What can a three-year-old possibly know of pictures?

Farther up the valley at Senovia's house, her mother opens the broad wooden gates and allows me to come in with a handful of children, now thinned out from the mile-long walk. I search through the photographs, then finally find it, a magical image from a day I photographed the family at work in their bean fields high up the slope. They are beside themselves with joy and pass it around as if it is manna from heaven. The old grandmother shuffles out from a dark interior, peering with teary, ancient eyes and smiling. It will be posted upon the wall or kept lovingly in a scrapbook under the bed.

The next day, hummingbirds dart above the Urubamba River to the buttercups that grow along the terraced embankments. Two white birds, egrets, I think, fly up the river as I cross the old Incan bridge at the edge of town. At the far end of the swaying bridge I meet a sad-eyed *viejita* (old woman). She sits on her haunches in the dust in front of an old Incan home of thatch and stone. When I stop to talk with her, I am riveted to her anguished eyes. The old woman takes off her battered, white top hat to show me that it, too, is poor and spent. I hold her hands in mine, hers that have toiled ninety years on the dry slopes above her little house, mine from a quite different world. Now, without a husband or other family, she waits in poverty for her death. She sits in dejection and I am drawn to simply sit with her for a few minutes, to share her grief that seems to have no beginning and no end. Her eyes are so watery and shapeless from crying that they are almost without form. I wonder if I, too, would be sad if my son had died and my wife had been drowned and my relatives had abandoned me and food were scarce and my clothes in tatters? I give her a handful of crumpled bills which she clutches like a ravenous hawk with gnarled, ancient hands. She weeps unabashedly.

Today I hike farther up along the tributaries of the Patacancha. Along the way I meet an exceptionally old Indian man driving gaunt goats before him with a switch. Passersby along the path whisper to me out of the old one's earshot that he is 120 years old. I ask the old man this, and he nods his head. Does he understand my Spanish, or does he know the one question that everyone seems to ask him? For surely, he is the oldest person I have ever seen. His old and twisted mouth voices Quechua sounds from another era. His name is Siprien Futuri and he lives near the small settlement of Pallata. This much I can understand in his half Quechua, half Spanish. Yet even with a load of wood on his back and the task

of driving goats, he is surprisingly agile and fit. His creased and lined face projects wisdom and clarity. I walk with him until Pallata, bid him adieu with a handshake and a smile, and continue up a few miles to a settlement of six houses called Colcoriqui.

Midsummer in the Andes is not warm by any means. A cold wind blows off the glaciers up near Huilloc. I pass beds of hardy winter wheat, high as my waist, called *trigo*, that will be used for summer breads by all these farming families. Nearing a bend in the path, I come upon an old man in his sixties at work irrigating his corn and wheat. He walks with me on the raised mud pathways he has so carefully constructed. We speak easily, the two of us, about the weather and the shortages of food year after year. He is worried and raises his eyes to the heavens as if to supplicate for the end of this cycle of scarcities. But he is proud of what he grows and takes a handful of ripe wheat in his rough hands to show off the fine heads.

The farmer, whose name is Leonardo, invites me back to his house to take some *chicha* and food. Two of his children I know slightly from school, a six-year-old named Naide, and an eighteen-year-old by the name of Orfelia whose face draws me in like a moth to the light. She looks like a gypsy, the kind from storybooks who rides a white horse in the moonlight and steals the hearts of admirers. She smiles coyly at me. The mother, a pretty woman with long, black braids and well-shaped legs, brings me *chicha* and a bowl of still-warm potatoes, with a second bowl of freshly cooked spinach greens from her garden, tart and delicious. The family of four sits with me as I eat.

The Incan past lingers, even with families like Leonardo's who clearly are mestizo and not Indian. Leonardo has made a new wall

to enclose his pigs and chickens, a wall of mud and straw with a tiled rampart to hold off the eroding water. Into this thirty-foot-long wall he has set eleven trapezoid-shaped niches. It is typical of the Incan buildings of long ago which always had these spaces constructed for their special possessions, an urn, a comb and brush, perhaps a magic bone or feather.

Colcoriqui is the highest I will climb today. I will wait until good weather to go higher up into Marca Cocha, Huilloc, and Patacancha villages. I bid farewell to Leonardo. Sweet Orfelia with her ruddy complexion and sleek, black hair walks with me to the footbridge, little Naide holding onto my hand along the path. She has a watch eye, or lazy eye, and has a look of "crazy wisdom" about her—an interior beauty to match Orfelia's exterior loveliness.

Downriver I go from the waving sisters, along cattle trails and around sleeping bulls who lie directly on the pathway. Soon I pass a school in a meadow. This is the village they call Pallata, a ragtag cluster of nearly thirty poor-looking huts on a hillside. It looks like something out of Ethiopia or the Sudan, but very green and with thickets of dwarfed, leafy trees.

I pass fifteen men making adobe brick. Barefooted, they squish the brown earth between their toes, adding straw and water and casting the bricks, when the consistency is right, into wooden molds about a foot in length. These men are friendly but drunk, and something inside me makes me keep walking even though they hold glasses of drink for me to take and speak to me like their long-lost brother. I move along uncomfortably as their calls now become a bit unsweet. Are they offended? I think they are too far gone to know the subtleties of just having been snubbed. I have been to this village on several occasions, and I think I don't like it. How can I say this? My experience has taught me to hate

nothing, to cling with pleasure to nothing, to only take the middle road of non-attachment. It is best simply to say, this is Pallata, these are men at work with drink. The village is dirty; the children have a cast-off look. The wind is cold today.

I walk across the three logs that serve as a bridge to the village and up past a small household. They, too, invite me for food and drink. But I am bound for a sleep in the tall grasses, tired from my hiking in these high hills.

Flowers are everywhere along this trail up toward the ancient, pre-Incan ruins of Puma Marca—daisies, roses, buttercups, gladiolas, lilies, bachelor buttons. I rest, exhausted, breathing hard, and below me is a world of minutia, a veritable landscape of the hallucinogenic mind: minute succulents, red-capped mosses, tiny and spindly cacti, and spiny flycatcher plants, dewdrops like pearls on mint leaves, lattice work of a celery stalk, lichens, orange mosses, rivulets no bigger than thread descending to the sea, and mushrooms of fluted, corrugated bulbs.

At a high meadow, a full half-hour below the village of Pallata, I throw myself down upon the earth in tall, sweet-scented grasses. The sound of the roaring Patacancha can be heard, its white glacial waters remain freezing even in summer. The sun is hot on my tanned face. I nod in between sleeping and waking; the blossoms and the snowy peaks float in and out of reality.

When I awake and sit up, I notice not far off, under an apple tree, Orfelia gazing at me. She rests against the other side of the tree's trunk with her arms upon a low branch, her sheep some distance to the north. She is not looking at them, she is looking at me. How long has she been here? She and I gaze at each other, forty yards of sun and shade between us, and neither of us smiles nor turns away. We simply gaze at each other. At eighteen, Orfelia is a woman in body, spirit, and perhaps mind. She is stunning, her face dark and ruddy with a sweet, red mouth. I long to kiss her. I wanted to the very first time I laid my eyes upon her in Señora Angélica's classroom last October.

We stare. Neither of us panics or turns away to avert looking. In my mind, I go through a whole series of life experiences with her: making love, working beside her, raising children together. Sidhartha and Kamala. And then somewhere, conversations with Pocha filter into the dream, into that Sidhartha-fairytale-forest dream. "Remember," she advises me, "if you kiss a woman she will want to marry you. It's all or nothing, no halfway romancing."

I cannot marry an eighteen-year-old. And what would Orfelia do with all this—this me? If I could steal a kiss or two or take a stroll in the moonlight with her, what then? How could I ever face Leonardo and his family again? I am bombarded by practicalities. I send these thoughts across to Orfelia through the winds. Maybe she receives them, for her face becomes pinched and tight, and she looks uncomfortable. I smile, but it is a social smile, an excuse, a mask. She does the same. She gathers up her shawl and white sack from the ground and heads off quickly to her strayed sheep. She looks embarrassed for having wished, too, for having gazed longingly at a gringo. I stand and head down the trail to town.

◆

CHAPTER SEVEN
<u> </u>

ONE MORNING I RECEIVE A MESSAGE
from one of the shaman Carbajal's teenage sons, a cryptic scrawl
on a napkin, something about
coming down to his compound
because the goods are in. I go immediately and find my friend propped
up in bed, smiling as always, with some fifteen customers waiting
in the spacious, stone room that serves as their bedroom. Carbajal
winks at me and then says he will be with me as soon as he is
through with a woman who sits on the edge of his bed. She has
lost her bull and has come to divine where it might be in the
myriad miles of hilltops. I watch as the old man throws the coca

leaves for her and intuits: Go to the bridge, then turn right and go up the hillside. You'll find your bull in a grove of eucalyptus trees. Fifteen *intis* (thirty cents), please. She takes matted old bills from under her soiled cuff, pays him, and departs.

Carbajal and I chat for five minutes about how things are going with the children, about my visits with the local people, and even about my friends and family back home. I love this man for his broken-toothed smile and twinkling eyes. He inquires whether I would enjoy being introduced to some new mountain spirits, the *apus* as they are called here. Of course, I say, especially since I am planning on trekking into the mountains soon to spend a few days in the Indian community called Huilloc.

Carbajal seems to know my plans, for he has been to Cuzco and has bought goods at a sorcerer's shop for an offering which I can make. Seashells, flowers, rice, grains, tobacco, sage, cedar, sugar, animal crackers, seeds, bread, bells, balls, a cross, tinsel, salt, anise, beans, raisins, feathers, twenty-two items each wrapped individually with paper, then all wrapped up together to form one packet. I am to go into the mountains and burn the packet on a high boulder under the sky, and to pour the remaining anise over the ashes in a ritual ceremony. He tells me that a place called Hosutpampa would be suitable, near Huilloc, the smoke being able to drift off to the four directions.

In the early afternoon I borrow a white horse from Carbajal and go into the mountains. One of Carbajal's sons walks with me to return the horse. We arrive in the cold light, at nearly ten thousand feet, at a place of great beauty where I burn the packet in honor of spending time in the *apu's* territory. No bolts of lightning, no portents of rattlesnakes and encircling condors, no stars shoot across the sky. All is quiet save for the wind that sweeps about my face with a cold hard pull. I say who I am and what I wish to grow toward, and ask for guidance and support along the way. I simply let it flow out upon the winds, one brief prayer among those of five billion other human beings on this planet.

The boy returns to Ollanta with the horse, and I continue upwards on foot with my pack, up along the Patacancha toward Huilloc, the Indian village where most of the Indians frequenting Ollanta come from, three more hours into the mountains. I don't know any Indians as yet, certainly not their names and their habits, though I am acutely aware of their smells, and faces, and bright red costumes, and even how they walk or sit in doorways. Often along the trails I notice my reserve in greeting them, thinking that they are less interested in a gringo than in one of their own kind. I want to see their village and their lifestyle, cast eyes through my telephoto lens at the high *chacras* of potatoes on the far distant slopes, and meet the children.

The trail is a pleasant gradual ascent, and I take time along the trek to visit with villagers in the dooryards or take *chicha* in the fields. A dog walks with me for several miles; we nap together by a small pool of cold water. When we awake, she heads home, and I up the trail, past an old, thatched, adobe church at a settlement called Marca Cocha and on to the high *altura* where trees give way to the great rolling steppes. At about four o'clock I come to Huilloc, a cluster of twenty thatched-roof, stone houses on a small pampa, or plain.

Huilloc is a typical *ayllu*, or community, often described as a clan of extended families living together in a clearly defined area with a communal sharing of land, animals, and crops. The *ayllu* was the basic social unit of the Incas, an early collectivist practice, present in the Andes long before the Quechua-speaking peoples rose to power and ruled over one-quarter of South America. The early *ayllus* were highly systematized, each person ruled by an elected leader (*mallcu*) and guided by a council of old men (*amutas*). It is most likely that one of the earliest groups in Peru, the Chavín, had *ayllus*, as did the other cultures that sprang up: the Paracas, the Mochicas, the Tiahuanaco, and the Chimú.

People have been watching me, as six women and three men approach from the north, the women laughing and greeting me with *Allinllachu*, how are you? Two of the women, middle-aged with ponchos and tall, pancake hats, take ocher from bags about their waists and with beautiful laughter smear my face with six or seven long lines, telling me in their own way that I am initiated into carnival.

I set up my tent in the sheep pasture beside the village school, and small boys come out from nearby houses and sit watching me as I connect the shock-corded tent poles together. A gossamer house of red nylon is made from a tiny, compressed sack. They put their heads into the tent, touch the material with sooty, little hands; I let six go in and they sit like stone statues. Scratchy music shatters the silent, mountain air, and I cock my head inquisitively and silently to ask the children where it comes from. The children point to a cluster of houses across the stream and lead me there by a stone bridge.

We approach a gathering of nearly thirty men and women on a hillside. The red color alone under the heavenly sky and roan cliffs speaks to me of ancient times. I screw up my courage and make my way to a man who seems to have the presence of an *alcalde*, or mayor. He seems delighted that I have come and immediately

introduces me in elementary Spanish to several of his male friends who shake my hand profusely. *Chicha* is offered in what is perhaps the dirtiest cup I have ever seen. It actually looks like a candlestick holder. I nearly decline, but decide perhaps the alcohol in the drink will kill the deadliest germs. I accept, quaffing the milky fluid in five swallows, my eyes riveted on the black, dirty sides that expose themselves like an emptying toilet bowl. *Salud papitos, salud amigos.* (Cheers little fathers, cheers friends.) They fill up the cup again and again, four times. They laugh and slap me on the back.

I move to the group on the hillside and sit with them, a bit inebriated already from the brew. One woman points up to the top of an enormous mountain, a mile or so away, and tells me that dancers are there and that they will be coming down soon. I squint my forty-six-year-old eyes and indeed behold, on a ridge a long way off, a thin line of red humans, like ants, descending along the trail.

There is a table in front of us where the *alcalde* and a priest or shaman of some kind bestow blessings upon the twelve men assembled there. *Chicha* is served to each, then petals of flowers are festooned on their heads, and finally two women from a nearby house bring each a bowl of meat and corn. On the small, hand-hewn table are peaches with flower blossoms stuck into their meaty pulp, each about a foot from the other. One man has fallen over backwards from the bench, drunk, and lies sprawled out in the very position in which he fell, arms akimbo, head facing skyward.

In the distance, nearly a mile up on a ridge trail near the path to Yanahuara, the line of ant-like humans in red advances. For a full half-hour we watch them, until they are overhead on a precipitous cliff trail, poised, as if ready to swoop down like birds. Thirty young men and youths wear white wings against their red costumes, and long tassels flow down their backs from their headdresses. My heart flies up to meet them; I am instantly with them in spirit. Drum and flute players come first, sweeping down the steep, cliff trail with the bird dancers racing behind, white arms outstretched, screaming some high-pitched chant that sounds like war cries.

The runners descend amid cheers and shouts from all of us gathered below, then, when they are down, we encircle them and give them wooden bowls of *chicha* and plates of food. They sweat, faces shining in the late-afternoon sun, and smile. My skin turns to goose bumps, the hair on the back of my neck stands up, and I run up and congratulate these jubilant young athletes.

Soon after, the bird dancers begin to assemble to continue their run to another cluster of houses a half-mile away. I am asked to join them and gladly accept, forgetful of altitude and its effect on my body. Happily I position myself between two friendly runners. We speed now like a Chinese dragon, twisting and shouting Quechua chants, flying over stone bridges. I leap down from one bridge and snap away with my camera as the runners pass overhead. The head runner, in charge of inspiring the others, passes above and throws me down a llama-hair whip as a symbol of friendship. I attach it around my waist, scramble up the embankment, and take up the last position in the advancing, surging line.

We run slowly through the now-chilled, shadowy valley, across stone bridges, the blue sky and far-distant peaks lit up in golden light. My lungs seem ready to burst, but my exhilaration in the spirit of shared companionship carries me on. Sweat rolls off my brow, the breathing from the young man in front of me is like song, and the drums and flutes pierce my senses.

We stop at a nearby settlement of thatched homes where a metal loudspeaker atop a tall, peeled pole blares out a powerful Quechuan tune, almost Islamic in sound, accompanied by a soprano-voiced woman wailing an incantation. In the courtyard twenty Indians, men and women, stand beside a record player with food and drink. They greet us with great shouts of joy and praise. I am offered clear alcohol from a musselshell by a proud, old man. I pour a few drops upon the earth before drinking, noticing that my new friends approve of the offering to *Pachamama*, then quaff the bitter brew.

Men and women begin to dance to flutes and drums, as the disco player and its car battery are shut down. The women's faces are smudged with ocher and streaks of black coal dust; in the eerie light from the candles their faces almost scare me, like masks. With their smooth, brown, bare legs, many crinoline skirts, and red, flannel streamers cascading down from their upside-down-colander hats, they are alluring to us men. Through the droning music and alcoholic haze I dance with Dorinda, a woman with an open smile, her dark, inviting eyes illuminated by the flickering light.

The women carry small llama-hair whips in their hands and judiciously castigate the men at their ankles during the dance. We are, it seems, allowed to jump over the whipping, something not easily done. The women are proficient at the whip, and it becomes both a masquerade of submission and sexual abandonment. Someone hands me a long, jagged weed to whip Dorinda's smooth curvaceous legs, but it is a fireweed of stinging nettles and the joke is on me, for I jump higher from its pain than from the whip of my partner.

I dance and drink until the world turns too quickly and the fine, night sky seems to swim in an unfamiliar orb. At dusk, a magic, orange glow has come to this tiny valley of thirty houses. Indians now become almost black as they cross the fields with cows and children. Domingo, a handsome youth of twenty who is one of the bird dancers, still in his costume, approaches in the twilight and invites me home for supper with him and his family. I follow gladly as I have brought only peanut butter, chocolate bars, a small bag of granola, and coffee. I am hungry from the day and the smell of cooking food is compelling.

Baskets and tools hang from the rafters, and the glow of their small fire illuminates his wife Simeona and a small boy of three seated upon the hearth. She, too, is handsome in her red blouse with hundreds of buttons and her colander hat sitting at a jaunty angle connected by a chin strap of intricate beadwork. Simeona gets up and serves me a bowl of thick soup and fried potatoes and a plate of cooked greens and steaming corn. We make little or no conversation, content to smile and watch the little boy called Benigno eating his meal with his fingers.

I wander out to my tent and lie in the inky darkness on a huge flat stone, watching the stars and listening to the music from the four settlements. At these elevations and so far from the smokestacks of Lima, the night sky has a brilliance unknown to those who live by street lamps in smoggy cities. I lie awake a long time, watching for UFOs, praying in my heart to have a message from these faraway stars. But the night belongs to the dancers and the disco players. I sleep fitfully throughout the night, the scratchy tunes like itchy sand in my ears, the heat lightning from the jungle making weird hallucinogenic tapestries of the surrounding peaks.

In the morning, sunshine falls softly upon my face, and roosters crow from all over the village. I turn toward the mountains and spot nearly thirty columns of blue smoke rising into the air from small homes high above me on the mountain slopes. If it were not for the smoke I wouldn't be able to distinguish the tiny houses from the vast, amorphous landscape. I see Simeona milking her cow, and, holding up a bag of coffee, tell her we can make *café con leche*. She shoots me a bright smile and continues milking.

Inside, Simeona grinds dried beans on a stone slab with quick, dextrous motions of her strong hands. Domingo makes *tostada de maiz*, slightly roasted corn kernels, which he adds to the simmering bean drink. I offer my coffee and soon a delicious morning beverage is served. Simeona is on her knees by the fire of smoky twigs, blowing through a metal pipe to bring oxygen to the coals. Fried eggs and potatoes are cooked, and while I eat Domingo asks me if I will be the godparent to their younger boy, a one-year-old

they call Tomás, someone I don't even know exists. They smile and point through the smoky darkness to their bed. I walk across and adjust my eyes to the light, beholding a fat, brown face with a head of profuse, black, curly locks. Small, black hands reach through the darkness and pull at my cheeks. He coos like a dove upon seeing me, and I adore him. Tomás will indeed be my god-child. Later in the day Domingo and Simeona cook up guinea pigs and a special soup. I am still revolted by eating these rodents, but accept the custom as part of the ritual. We eat a ceremonial meal, complete with huge bottles of beer, in honor of Tomás' first hair cutting and eventual baptism.

In Huilloc, villagers depart on narrow, cliff trails early in the morning to gather wood with their horses or to walk to their fields with their digging tool, the *taclla*, to tend their potatoes and corn. They all wear the gorgeous, red costumes, high collars festooned with multi-colored buttons, and Amish-style black hats with broad brims. The children are very shy and speak little or no Spanish, their voices high and sweet as small bells. Everyone has dirty hands and coarse, callused feet. They work hard in the fields and in the nuturing of their animals, especially the llamas and alpacas from which their clothing is made. There are no stores and the villagers are quite self-sufficient. It is a simple life. The people go to bed with the sun and get up with the sun.

I spend three days in Huilloc, getting to know the villagers, helping Domingo and Simeona harvest their potatoes and gather firewood on the mountain slopes. I like working with the family, hard though it is upon my body, unaccustomed to the high elevation of nearly thirteen thousand feet. With Domingo today, I haul down a huge pine tree that is too far up on a ridge for their horse to skid out. He and I work two hours pulling it down the scree slopes, sweat pouring down our faces, the rough bark cutting my hands.

With Simeona, I gather potatoes high up in the mountains, bent over for hours at a stretch, until my back feels broken, too proud and too in awe of Simeona's strength to object to the pain. Often I look after the boys while their parents work. We spend long hours playing in my tent where they like to rummage through my things, especially the bag of granola; both Benigno and Tomás love the tamari-roasted almonds. Occasionally I photograph them with the Polaroid camera. They are fascinated with their own images.

One Huilloc afternoon, the weather holding fine, I hike out of the village far to the north, up, up, up toward the high pass where the llamas are shepherded. Far below, the houses are draped in a cold, black shadow by three o'clock, so steep are these Andes. I walk very slowly, feeling the altitude's effect on my heart and lungs and sometimes my aching head. I must not hurry. Walking slowly, I get to watch these mountain farmers: children with sheep on hillsides and women with hand scythes cutting bright green fodder for stabled calves.

Coming to a plateau where I least suspect habitation, I am surprised to find four thatched houses with nearly forty villagers lazing in the late-afternoon sun. The snow-capped Andes are a stunning backdrop for the final day of carnival. Women and babies lie on the grass, old men sit and drink *chicha*, and boys and girls play tag. I spend three hours with these new people, dancing and drinking. My face is smeared with ocher on several occasions by pretty women. I reciprocate friendship by taking Polaroids which I judiciously label with their names and dates. I present these portraits to the older people, much to the lament of the younger ones. There are no gringos here, though it is a mere four-hour walk from the train station.

Living in my tent and taking my meals with Simeona and Domingo allows me to observe old Incan life firsthand. They laugh sometimes at my enthusiasm over something as common to them as making a digging implement from the hip bone of a deer that Domingo has shot. I sit by the hearth on a stone slab, and slowly eat my gruel or hold little Tomás or Benigno and watch Simeona grinding her corn or cooking soup. Simeona is a highly capable Indian woman, strong like her husband, and a loving, gracious mother.

Two young schoolteachers come by today, women in their early twenties, and sit with us, sharing the late-afternoon sunlight that slants through the cloud-filled skies. Petra and Teresa seem happy to make the acquaintance of a *yanqui* and take special interest in two pieces of clothing I have, fleecy jackets, one of cobalt blue and the other of electric red. They touch the soft, wool-like synthetic with obvious delight. I let them try them on, and even invite them to wear them for the night, something they want to do because it is very cold.

A peddler comes by as we speak, a mestizo man from the Calca area who has traveled on horseback over the high sierras to sell broadcloth and notions to the villagers. At Domingo's promise to make me a pair of Indian pants, I buy three bolts of broadcloth from the gentleman, wonderful homespun wool that feels soft yet durable. Petra and Teresa help me measure the amount of cloth I need, holding up the bolt to their chins and stretching the cloth to their fingertips for measurement. I remove my khaki trousers for them to measure, standing in the cold in a pair of electric blue, Spandex running tights. Certainly the women and the Indians have never seen such cloth before and are mesmerized by it. I suppose I look like some psychedelic, fluorescent butterfly. There is much laughter and obvious jokes in Quechua, and I am glad when I can put on my khakis again. Within a half-hour, the women and Domingo and Simeona have fashioned a pair of homespun woolen pants that fit me perfectly.

A neighbor comes by before supper, a cousin to Domingo named Gabriel. He shakes hands with all of us still assembled in the courtyard and asks if I would honor his family by becoming the godparent to his eight-month-old daughter. The hair-cutting ceremony will take place in an hour. Can I come? Gabriel's face is so kind and earnest, I cannot refuse.

Gabriel and I leave immediately, trekking across the slopes of old Incan terracing in the fading light, past Indian women at work at their backstrap looms, weaving the fiery ponchos that protect their loved ones from cold and rain. On a hillock overlooking an agricultural valley we come to Gabriel's dark, little, thatched, mud-and-

stone house. His wife Leonarda, a woman of twenty-five, greets us at the smoky doorway, embracing me the half-hearted Indian way, shoulders rubbing against each other, faces almost touching.

She speaks no Spanish but points to her badly swollen cheek, which she instructs me in Quechua is in great pain from an infected tooth. I reach into my rucksack and extract some aspirin and a small bottle of codine, giving them to her as a housewarming gift. She turns and places the medicines on a shelf by the fire, then sorts out her baby, Dora, from among her seven children on the hearth rug. I am given a seat by the fire, and upon my lap sits little Dora, bare-bottomed and sweet-faced, bewildered and frightened by surely the first white person she has ever seen. Her eyes are wide and search the whole room for the familiarity of her brothers and sisters who speak softly to her in Quechua.

A gentle rain suddenly appears and diminishes what little light comes through the open doorway. An old grandmother cooks by the fire while I play with Dora's fat, little legs. Gabriel sits in a rickety chair at the door's entrance and inscribes Dora's name, age, and date in the family Bible. It suggests a deeply moving photograph, and I am drawn to recording it. It speaks to me so much of South America and this mysterious mountainland in the clouds: a father in mud-caked pants and broken sandals sitting in a rickety chair with legs outstretched, the soft, amber-brown light of evening upon his hands and face as he inscribes the torn pages of the Bible; his six-year-old son standing serenely at his side and watching his father write.

This is the one-hundredth generation upon the land, and yet another child who will toil incessantly his entire lifetime for food and water and shelter and a place called home. Despite all—the revolution, the road that never came, the absence of doctors and nurses, the broken sandals and the mud-caked doorway—another Quechua speaker, a girl called Dora, has come.

◆

CHAPTER EIGHT
─────────────────

I HAVE COME AGAIN TO CUZCO WITH ROCIO, TO GET MORE FUEL for my primus stove. The so-called fuel I bought in Urubamba turns out to be a mixture of *pisco* and *chicha* which understandably clogs the fuel line. It is typical, this ordering one thing and getting another. It wears you down very fast.

This morning in Cuzco there are two tanks in the Plaza de Armas. They sit like poison toads, ready to spit death from their mouths upon anything that threatens to disrupt the tranquility of the summer morning. From a shoeshine man, Roberto, Rocío and I learn that the guerrillas near Cuzco have been apprehended with as much as two hundred pounds of dynamite. One well-placed load will, of course, cream a busload of tourists like an H-bomb, and tourists from around the world will stop coming. This the

government knows, and this the government cannot afford to let happen, ever. We walk past the tanks, our veins boiling with this harsh reality of South America.

The *Sendero Luminoso*, Shining Path, are extreme, leftist guerrillas who are strongest in the neighboring state of Ayacucho. They offer to the campesinos and Indians a Maoist-type ideology that seems on the surface appealing and closer to the old Incan ways than that of the current leader, Alán García and his APRA party. But time is running out for Garcia and company, and if the *Sendero Luminoso* doesn't topple them, two other parties await in Lima's wings, the United Left and a right-wing Social Christian Party.

We walk the Avenida del Sol to the post office to mail letters and come upon a protest march of perhaps two hundred people, men and women carrying banners and placards with anti-government slogans. A brave, old campesina, in her seventies, wearing a skirt and colorful red shawl, leads the protest march, her Peruvian flag held proudly above her head. This group of farmers seems desperate, bent on bringing the Lima government to its senses even if they have to walk the full six hundred miles on foot to the capital. Years of lies, years of waiting on the promises of schools, hospitals, electricity, roads, and fair prices for their harvests, have taken their toll.

I move into the street to photograph the old campesina, but fall back, embarrassed. I cannot take her picture. She doesn't know who I am or whom I represent or where the picture will eventually end up. I cannot for a single instant take the chance that my actions would increase her worry and fear. As far as she's concerned, undoubtedly, the picture could end up in the files of the Guardia Civil's memory bank.

Roberto and Rocío tell me that about twenty years ago sweeping land reforms called *La Reforma Agraria* returned the majority of the land to the people after nearly four hundred years. Up until that time, all land, except for the highest mountaintops and the driest deserts, belonged to the church, the government, the military, and the rich, ruling families. The concept of the old Incan *ayllu* providing for every citizen was abolished by the Spanish, who ordained that one-half of all produce would go to them. Under penalty of death, the church and the Spanish warlords held the people in slavery. The church cast gold effigies of Jesus Christ and kept the Indians and campesinos on the brink of starvation, with an early pitiless death in the mines as their penance. Fifteen million people perished in the dreadful mines, all under the auspices of the church. Now, the guerrillas are back to steal the land again in a new way. Rocío casts a sorrowful eye. All the more reason, Roberto says, for us to build the clinic—a ray of light in the enveloping darkness.

I part company with Rocío and Roberto and head back to Ollanta. On the ride from Pisac back to town, about twenty of us are riding along in an open truck when bands of youths along the road begin hurling buckets of water at us. It is carnival month here in Peru. The people celebrate all month long by throwing water at each other and hurling flour into people's faces, always with a sense of mirth. It is late in the afternoon and the air is chilled by our speeding truck. The water drenches us often and we see little humor in carnival festivities. We want to get home, we are cold and hungry. Often we try to duck the onslaught of spray.

A young mother and her three-year-old daughter and I are the only ones who react to a group up the road poised with buckets. We three immediately scrunch down in the truck to hide, and the long seconds of waiting are both endless and endlessly delicious, as our three heads touch and our hands hold each other's, and our breathing becomes as one. It is just us three on the floor with anxious eyes and mingled breath and clenched hands. The water comes, we miss the drenching, and resume our positions with the wind blowing in our faces. We don't acknowledge anything between us, not even exchange glances. It has been us three, a marriage, a lifetime, a simple coupling of three spirits. I savor those seconds for the rest of the ride home.

One night during carnival I watch a dozen boys, probably around ten and eleven years old, attack with flour a sweet, eleven-year-old girl sitting with her mother selling cabbages. The boys unmercifully run raids on her and throw flour into her face, and also upon her mother. I run after the boys to chase them away. I even pick up the cruelest of the boys and turn him upside down momentarily,

threatening, mockingly, to pulverize his head into the stone street. I cool down, release him, and walk to the woman and daughter to see if they are all right. I am not a physically abusive person. I am deeply embarrassed. I go immediately to Doña Eva's store and buy twelve Sublima chocolate bars and go to each boy and speak with them and shake their hands and learn their names. They hold no resentment. On my way back to my pension, I look closely at what just happened. What was I really doing out there, protecting good in the face of evil? Does violence justify violence? And am I, a foreigner, to be the judge of what is good and bad here?

As the water-throwing of carnival month continues, I watch from my pension window daily as villagers—some well into their fifties—stand waiting for the unsuspecting open trucks that pass by, dousing them with buckets of water, laughing hysterically and not caring a hoot for the often disparaging remarks they get in response. Even in Ollanta we all think our everyday, formal posture is the only acceptable one. Carnival's water-throwing—balloons and buckets—brings out a totally different reality. Whack! No matter how important you think you are, you are soaked through and through. In that ridiculous soaking can come an awakening, granted a small one, an unraveling of who you think you are.

Tonight I play my cassette player outside for the first time in my long stay here. I have kept it in my room and played soft music like the Paul Winter Consort and Pat Metheny to accompany the moon's ascent on the Temple of the Moon, and sometimes crisp rock-and-roll when I come back from a cold shower to get me moving in the morning. But I have refrained from playing it in public, probably because I have sentiments about not setting an example of material opulence for these villagers. Once you begin to accumulate material goods, there almost seems no turning back from it. In part, that is why I am here, to divest myself of the outer trappings. But this evening I play my boom box for Pocha and Carlitos and the two kitchen girls, Abelina and Eli. The tape I choose is a Kitaro selection, New Age synthesizer music. We gather in the doorway where the flute-like sounds float out into the night like quicksilver, swallowed up by the trees and streams and people alike who have come close, like moths to the light. This Kitaro tape is far beyond language, or cognitive knowing. Soon fifty people laze upon the lawn in silence, mesmerized, transported to some distant place. Ten minutes, twenty minutes, a full hour of concert under the stars.

When the crowd has swelled to almost sixty, I feign an excuse that the gathering is too large for police regulations and move slowly away, toward the plaza and a group of teenagers gathered there. I engage them momentarily in talk about this machine from Japan, then casually slip in an amazing song by Peter Schilling called

"Major Tom," which is about some mythical lost-in-space as-tronaut gone beyond the beyond in outer space. It is a tune so riveting in its rock-orchestral arrangement that I never tire of hear-ing it, even after several hundred plays. I wonder if they will like it? I play it loudly, noticing the police station's doors are shut and the lights out. The chorus of the song immediately takes the teen-agers by storm. Now fifty kids are scurrying toward us. There are other tapes in town, but no one has "Major Tom." "Four, three, two, one, earth below us, spinning, falling. . . ." We play the song twenty times in a row, and we fly, literally fly in spirit as a group, somewhere very high and wide and beautiful. When it comes to an end, we all just stand around the machine smiling at each other.

In late summer heat, with lightning and thunder in the upper valleys, I hike up along the trail to the pre-Incan ruins of Puma Marca. In afternoon light I enter a steep ravine with cascading waterfalls among tall eucalyptus groves, with an abandoned shepherd's cabin high on a hill. The forest is cool and green, mys-terious. It gives off delicious smells of lemon mint and wild roses, eucalyptus, wild geraniums, and damp sphagnum mosses. Birds sing sweetly in the thickets, the wind is up in the leaves. Up I trudge, high into the mountains, into the clouds themselves, it seems. On the opposite side of the valley, white specks—cattle—make their own trails far higher than mine. The valley is now feathered in greens and blacks at dusk. Long shadows tear the peaks like knives. I turn back regretfully as the light dims; footing is pre-carious on these mountain trails. At a creek crossing, Indians come by on horses with gear. In the soft light they look like apparitions.

Not far below I come upon two children whom I know, a brother and a sister named Victor and Lurdis. They are bedding down in the *chacra* fields with their mother and father and brothers and

sisters to guard their crop of ripe corn. Robbers from the cities often strip cornfields and sell the produce. Crops to these villagers are life, and many a night families and their faithful little watchdogs sleep out in tiny straw shelters. Victor and Lurdis take my hands and lead me over walls, now pitch dark, to a small, yellow fire where the family rests in a circle with their goats and their dogs. The mother, a woman named Albertina who wears coarse, ragged clothing and a white hat, gives me a plate of food.

Little Victor blows on the fire, his cheeks like red bellows, close to the ground. His older brother, dressed in rags, lights a small lantern and hangs it from a projection on the huge boulder nearby. Lightning and thunder commence, and the old father looks at the heavens to assess what their night will be. There is the smell of corn leaves, and meat cooking on sticks, with little talk and a soft, priestly voice offering mass from a portable radio.

Later that night, a full moon rises over the ruins of Ollanta, a blood red, creamy orb poking out from behind Pinculluna onto the altar of the Temple of the Sun. I steal out of town almost on tiptoes as the village prepares to sleep, to a hole in the wall where I ease toward the moonlit base of the ruins, with its shadowy heights of quarried stone flooded in silence. I walk quietly through the ruins, running fingers along the smooth edges of the cut stone. When I reach the top, the throne seat of the Sapa Inca himself waits in the red moonlight. Soon I am lying down on a giant stone slab, cold as a crypt, and fall easily asleep. Awaking a bit later and still lying on my back, I watch the starry heavens. Around me, the gardens of stone are like a fabled city, dormant and sleeping, waiting for the return of its citizens to take up the vigil of prayerful life again.

◆

CHAPTER NINE

I HAVE POSTPONED MAKING THE TWO-HOUR RIDE TO MACHU Picchu for too long now. Everyone has already gone. The Germans, the French, the Americans, even the Peruvians have gone. Why have I lingered so long, and why do I labor with the thought of joining the crowds? Is it the train ride, that horror of horrors? In my mind there is some association with Disney World, paying money and standing in line to view some lifelessly animated, fake scenery. At least Machu Picchu is not some phony Hollywood set; it is the archaeological wonder of this continent, the lost city of the Incas. I will go tomorrow.

I am in luck this morning, as an unexpected, sparkling clean, tourist train stops at Ollanta's rail station with one seat unaccounted for. The train's five cars are filled with European and North Amer-

ican tourists, with a few Japanese. The valley flows by at thirty miles per hour, a magnificent view of mountains and a turbulent Urubamba River. Twice we see white-water-rafting groups in giant inflatables, each raft with its complement of adventuring tourists in colorful life preservers. Their faces express fear and timidity, and well they should, for nearly every year there is a death or two on this raging river.

Towns along the rails change in appearance. I have not been this close to the jungle before, and the land lies differently here, more dense vegetation, palms and hanging vines and villagers with tall rubber boots and machetes. We pass through Aguas Calientes, the town one mile before the gates of Machu Picchu. It is a dismal place, even in the clear sunlight. There is no grass or greenery, the trees have been cut down, and the streets and lots are merely packed mud and rubble. It has a dead feeling, as if the villagers here had long ago sold their souls. I am glad that our train does not stop.

The train screeches to a halt at the gates of Machu Picchu, and we three hundred crane our necks upward through the clean windows to see if we can see the fabled lost city of the Incas. But no, we cannot, and are directed by impersonal guards to cue up in lines for the buses that will take us a half-hour up the mountain to the city. Two long hours we wait in lines, a dilapidated old bus coming every now and then and slaking off a handful of the now disgruntled visitors. People are smoking all around me; they chew their filter tips as if they were masticating meat, and it's their way, I guess, of coping with the hated delay. I am not doing that well myself. Finally the bus takes me, and upward we go on a tortuous, mountain switchback of gravel.

The site is twenty football stadiums' worth of quarried stone steps and small houses without roofs, courtyards leading to shrines, terracing that stretches to the crest of a hill. A full mile below, the mighty Urubamba River snakes its way toward the Amazon jungle. An enormous hotel with an outdoor veranda holds several hundred gawking tourists who seem to be enjoying the views of the amazing city. I enter the gates where a wizened, old Indian man close to eighty takes my ticket and looks deeply into my face as if to unearth whether in this nine millionth visitor there is a spark of knowing. With eyes sunk far back into his head, and old leathery skin, he is in charge of the gates of Machu Picchu, the gatekeeper to this site's spirit. Roberto has told me that I should get to know him, that he has been known to open the gates at dark for the right gringos to prowl around, to do LSD in the moonlight, to meditate at the Temple of the Sun. I look deeply into his eyes for some sort of sign. Nothing. Then two German women behind me interrupt my revery and make it known that I am lingering. Move along, they seem to say. I move on.

I enter the sacred grounds of one of the most fabled cities in the entire world, only to find my attention riveted on hundreds of other tourists, climbing above and below like ants. I walk through this fortified city, my head pounding with disarray, confusion, and distaste for my fellow tourists. "Hey, Gertrude," someone yells from above me on the stone terracing. "Betcha can't fit your fat ass through this Inca doorway."

These people have made a costly pilgrimage here, scrimped and saved up their hard-earned money in a cookie jar for a once-in-a-lifetime trip to something beyond the shopping mall, Las Vegas, and their everyday lives. Why do I begrudge them being here, too?

I sleep on a high, grassy knoll overlooking the ruins. Though clouded by my own distaste for the mobs, I am staggered by this ancient city of quarried stone. Each step, each house lintel, each

curved wash basin is exquisitely smooth and perfectly finished. It was the pinnacle of Incan architecture and spiritual learning, a hidden city that eluded even the conquistadors. Overlooking the entire city, a needle-like spire thrusts high into the sky, a mountain they call Huayna Picchu. I can see a handful of old houses there, clinging to the cliffs, a place where these Incas went for spiritual strength and wisdom. Then why is it that I can't get in touch with my own true self here? Many times in my travels I find that the most famous spots seem empty, as if the spiritual powers have moved on to some unknown spot where mystery still dwells. After three hours of trying I come away from the ruins with a feeling of confusion and sadness, and a sense of emptiness and loss.

Rocío and I have made the trip to Cuzco again, to see Roberto, but more importantly to see Benito. He is an old man and will not last forever. We have received word that the government has been spying on him, posting plainclothes guards near his street to see who comes, who goes, and what is going on. Perhaps the jealous drunkards of his dirty village wish to silence his spiritual voice. Perhaps the government thinks Benito is working with the *Sendero* subversives. Who knows?

The guerrilla problem increases daily. There are tanks in the square again this morning when Rocío and I meet Roberto at the Wisfala Café. It is early morning; the tanks must have spent the night in the plaza holding off any threats by the *Sendero Luminoso*. Both Rocío and Roberto are tense this morning, knowing they are interlopers here in Peru, merely guests of the government, passing through. Both have temporary visas, Rocío's is long overdue. Over coffee, eggs, and yogurt, Rocío tells us she has made plans to return to Spain soon, to renew her visa, and to gather medical supplies for our health clinic in Ollanta. She tells Roberto that her

plane leaves in the afternoon, and that before she goes she wants to see Benito in Huasao, to get his blessing.

Roberto is dressed in brown this morning; he looks tired and confused. The usual clarity in his eyes is gone. He drinks four cups of coffee to "jump start my mind," laughing a little as he says this, but even his humor is weak this morning. He looks impatient and frustrated and is certainly not the self-confident Roberto. His quest for a higher consciousness and the invisibility of true self seems to have temporarily stalled. Still, he tries to be affable and squeezes Rocío to assure her that all is well, that the clinic is still happening, that Peru is here to stay.

After breakfast, a soft-spoken man approaches us, gives Roberto a warm embrace, and speaks to Rocío and me in Spanish. He is Alejandro, a shaman from the jungle, from a vine-covered province called Madre de Dios, Mother of God. He has spent the night at Roberto's apartment in San Blas. Roberto mentioned him briefly at breakfast. This Alejandro is a gentle man of sixty, the chief of his small village near the headwaters of the Amazon. He has come to Cuzco on a rare visit for supplies, but also for other, mysterious reasons which, although alluded to, are unknown even to Roberto. It may have to do with seeing Benito, a counterpart of Alejandro's spiritual world. But who knows what lies in the mind of a shaman? I once spent time in the jungles of Guatemala and would visit with a shaman who always had a boa constrictor around his neck, and never once did the old man tell me why he had the snake hanging on him.

We walk together, Rocío and Roberto, Alejandro and I, past the tanks, toward the market. Alejandro, despite his neat, city attire of pressed slacks, clean white shirt, and shined shoes, is not at home in the city and refuses to talk. Roberto tells us about this man. At home, he and his people wear scanty clothing—or none—and live a life purposefully far removed from the trappings of modern society. Much of the villagers' time is spent in trancelike states, where the jungle hallucinogen *ayahuasca* elevates them to other planes of consciousness, where they are transported from one bank of the huge, brown river to the other bank in the belly of a giant watersnake, where man-sized river fish sing sad, plaintive songs which Alejandro's people understand and love. These stories excite Roberto. He suggests that we go to see Benito, the shaman, right away. A cab is hailed, arrangements made by Roberto in fluent Spanish, and off we speed in a beat-up, old Plymouth.

Benito is sick when we get there, his other-worldly eyes clouded over with a veil of mist and mucus. Rocío moves quickly through the packed-mud courtyard and bends down to examine him, anxiety on her beautiful face. She opens her small, black bag and takes out her stethoscope and listens to the old man's heart. Nate, the half-crazed wife and apprentice to the old sorcerer, stands nearby, with her head half-cocked like a worried chicken.

Benito is too sick to throw the coca leaves for Rocío. He sits slumped in the corner like an expiring fish in the bottom of a rowboat. Roberto pulls closer, to whisper in Benito's ear some message, perhaps about bringing Alejandro here to meet him. Benito listens without much interest, taking off his wristwatch with awkward movements and giving it to Roberto. Is this some meaningless gesture, or is there symbolism here? Before my mind can find the answer, Roberto is motioning for Alejandro to draw close, to meet the old shaman.

I watch as Alejandro approaches Benito, bending down on supple legs and touching the old man's hands. Alejandro pulls out a small

headress of yellow cockateel feathers and puts it on—albeit crooked—as if to correctly introduce himself. Benito seems to come to life, pulling himself up as best he can to a more upright position, old bones laboring with the work of his huge weight. They speak in a language I do not know. They are warriors of the spirit world, one receiving his teachings from the plants of the jungle, and the other receiving his magic from the mountain spirits of Ausangate, or *apus*, as Benito likes to call them. The jungle meeting the mountains. They clasp hands and Benito slouches back against the wall.

We stay only a few minutes, Nate taking charge of the courtyard and almost pushing us all out the door, protecting her husband. She seems bitter today, her craziness more like aggressiveness, the claws of a hawk protecting her young. We understand. Benito is dying.

That afternoon in Cuzco, Roberto and I take Rocío to the airport to catch her connecting flight to Lima, and then homeward to Madrid. She cries, and we linger with her on the crowded floor near the departure gate until the last minute. It feels like we will never meet again, but we know this is not true. She will be back in a month or two, and by then the land for the clinic will have been secured and construction started on the new buildings there. Still, something is not right with Rocío and her going. I don't know what it is. The boarding announcement comes again, we hug and kiss for the final time, and then she is gone.

To shake off the blues, Roberto takes me to meet two eccentric friends of his, both street people. The first is a man who lives alone on the streets, on the Avenida del Sol, the ancient Incan road of the kings. His name is Barás; he is probably fifty, though it's hard to know because he has abandoned the ordinary world and neither bathes nor shaves nor changes his clothing. He looks like a wild animal. Roberto says he isn't mad, just beyond caring whether he participates in civilized culture or not. Barás eats in the garbage pits of Cuzco, not daintily picking out select morsels, but shoving fistfuls of the gooey, rotten food into his mouth with reckless abandon. He also, Roberto says with a faint smile, plays with himself in public, masturbating underneath his baggy clothing as people walk past him. According to Roberto, nobody else ever talks to him, or befriends him, or even takes the time to look at him anymore. He is considered an animal, despised.

When I meet him with Roberto, he is lying down on the broad sidewalk of the avenue, with hundreds of people walking over and around him. We touch his arm gently, he looks up at us, his unfocused eyes swimming with crazy wisdom, and he calmly props up his head in his hand and greets us. He seems not wild, but quiet and calm. I find out in our five minutes with him that he is content to live the way he does. Things are going well in his life, he says. He likes himself, he likes the world. When we ask Barás if he wants some coffee and cake, he declines and tells us that he has just eaten. We leave him lying back down on the pavement, a dog sniffing his feces-caked pants.

That same evening, Roberto takes me to another homeless street person, a sack of bones weighing no more than ninety pounds. He is well into his seventies, with only three crooked teeth in his laughing head, and a sagging, ripped jacket and funny shoes with no laces, his gnomish, little monkey-body riddled with tuberculosis. His name is Lalílala. He plays the *zampoñas*, the early cane panpipe, and is considered the very best *zampoñas* player in all of Cuzco. He is outside the well-to-do Paititi restaurant making music in the misty night air, though no one stops to listen. Roberto has known Lalílala for years, having seen him as a younger man when he first came to Peru. Everyone laughs at him. The teenage boys beat him up regularly, stealing his ripped clothing, pissing on him as he sleeps in alleyways. He smiles with wild eyes at us and continues playing a haunting, Incan tune.

A cold wind blows, and the little man hunches up his bony frame and sways with the wind. I scamper off to the Paititi and return with a borrowed silver tray and three frosty *pisco* sours in glass goblets, and like a dignified waiter I serve Lalílala first, the host of our street serenade. We stay almost an hour, with me going back and forth with the silver tray to bring holy spirits to the holy gathering, now quite drunk and laughing hysterically. Finally Lalílala plays a triste, a sad song, and the panpipe whispers while the man hunches up his misshapen body, like death personified.

Lalílala has no money, no home, not much of a body, and no future. He has rhythm, though, and with his lilting eyes and mystical music he transports your spirit high above the earth. When I hug him goodnight, his bony body is so frail and sick, so tired and beaten down, that I think he is not there. He looks up at me with his three crooked teeth and his mystical eyes and we laugh and laugh. We hoot so loudly that people in the streets are forced to look. Crazies, druggies. "*Gate, gate, paragate, parasumgate bodhi Svaha.*" (Go, go, hurry quickly, cross over to the other shore.)

Needing some time alone, today I borrow Carbajal's white horse to ride in the high country above the ruins of Puma Marca. The old man laughs with his broken-tooth smile as I pull the cinch tighter on the mare, for he knows that I like to ride fast up in the *altiplano*. Does the sweat on her flanks when we return give away our secret? Or does the old, crazy shaman know because the winds tell him so? He seems not to mind that his white mare will move across the slopes at faster-than-usual speeds.

The mare, a four-year-old, is small and round, with a muscular chest and slender legs, narrower than mine at the ankles. She seems a cross between an Arabian, with her petite neck, small nose and head, and one of the South American blood-and-guts trail ponies of the Andean campesinos. The Spanish would have brought her ancestors here by ship a long, long time ago. As I ride out of the village, with Carbajal standing in the street on his crooked, wooden crutches smiling at me, I imagine what it must have been like for those first Indians to have seen horse and rider approaching. Reports from around the globe persist that people upon first seeing a human upon a horse believed it to be one terrifying beast, indivisible. Their fear was heightened when this beast started lopping off their heads.

Near Huilloc the landscape gives way to great, sweeping stretches of treeless *altiplano*. The white mare, who I call Blanco, speeds along the steppe in a surreal light under a saffron sky studded with elliptical clouds, like flying saucers hanging in the air. She seems to love these heights, too, and I hardly have to touch her flanks with my bare feet to get her to fly. I should not go so fast on this horse, but I love to fly like the wind, to give the animal its head and allow it to be transformed temporarily from a beast of burden into an animal charged with spirit and adventure.

Today she and I ride as one, fast, past the Indian houses and out onto the flat pampa. Llamas skitter out of the way as we fly by. Her barrel chest heaves and I feel the lunging of her powerful strides. With the coarse mane stinging my face, the world is turned dappled and ephemeral through my teary eyes. Faster and faster we ride, my legs gripping hot flanks, our breaths coming as one, my lips whispering to her—come on, come on. Then the river is in sight and there is the letting go, her legs moving slower and slower and stiffening and eventually stopping. I encircle her neck like a lover and kiss her.

There are gringos tonight at my pension. We sit drinking coffee and smoking cigarettes, discussing the Shining Path and their subversive activities against both the government and the country people. We are all concerned, as well we should be. If any of us daydreaming gringos are foolish enough to put ourselves within reach of these guerrillas, there is a strong chance of being abducted and held hostage. Ransom is the *Sendero*'s quick way of raising money for their cause.

A curly-haired German man of forty has heard through the gringo grapevine that a band of Finnish and Dutch hikers barely escaped with their lives up on the Inca Trail, near Kilometer 88. The *Senderos* left the gringos bereft of their money, passports, and camping gear with only their underwear to walk home in. Like the aftermath of a bad car accident, we gringos tonight affirm that we will take new steps of precaution and safety, especially when hiking near Machu Picchu. It is best, we agree, not to walk too far off the trail.

Just before retiring to bed, Pocha, while cleaning out the waste bins, finds a crumpled-up *Newsweek* magazine, an international edition barely a week old. She hands it to me as I make my way upstairs. By candlelight I read of another incident involving the *Senderos*. An American woman, traveling in the province of Ayacucho, heartland of the *Sendero Luminoso*, had been arrested and interrogated by the local police about a 1987 murder of two government officials. Despite her testimony that she had no allegiances to the *Senderos*, she was jailed in a Lima prison, in a four-story wing which the female inmates had taken over and turned into a *Sendero* training camp, complete with banners of Mao, Marx, and Lenin to proclaim the mighty revolution. Now four months later, she is reported as being taken to a new prison at an undetermined location, the government of Peru still unsure as to her innocence.

The *Senderos* are said to have murdered thousands already. Most of their attacks have been against government officials, police, and the military. Their hatred of both the Soviet Union and the United States has led to an all-out war to establish a workers' state along the lines of Mao Tse Tung's China.

In the morning I walk out of my pension toward the plaza to see if the children are playing. At the police headquarters, three policemen stand in the lighted doorway looking out at the plaza. I feel paranoid, thinking that they see within my rucksack my parapher-

nalia for taking pictures and writing down notes. I have had nothing to do with these men in all my months here.

These Ollanta policemen are the down-to-earth variety of human beings, pragmatic and forceful. Spiritualism and riding fast horses in the *altiplano* for kicks is not their style. They are fat and sour-faced, hiding behind their mirrored sunglasses and incessantly blowing whistles at passing trucks. My attire of shorts and sneakers with no socks may offend them. Mine is a world far apart from theirs, where bullets, bribery, and extortion prevail. Cristina and Alberto, my baker friends, tell me sad tales of Christian missionaries having been abducted in the night last year by these police, never to return. The children tell me that the police think I am strange, a lover of mute, old women and children who play tag. That's fine with me. I will play the fool. I hope that they won't shoot me then.

There are cockfights this Sunday morning. The church bells' incessant din calls worshipers to the altar of Christ, as the adobe bricks for the coming fights are being set up in an abandoned field behind my pension. It is a macabre sight, this ring of bricks, and the four rows of bleachers being built for the spectators. Granted, these are just roosters, lowly, dumb chickens. Still, they have their rights, their lives. Welcome to the Third World, I rationalize, where life is cheap, animal and human.

Pocha looks up from her washing in the veranda below and casts a sorrowful expression in my direction. We are silent with our feelings and I wonder if she feels her vulnerability as a woman. For what hope is there when men decide to sport with the defenseless? Pocha has cried many a night in her little room. I have heard her low wails time and again, and sometimes in the morning we talk about the husband who left her and who mistreated her. She laments that so many of the village women have the same story to tell. The roosters in the ring, and many of the village women, are alike, forced to endure the torment of men sick with some blind, perverse rage.

There is such cruelty in the world these days, even in Ollanta. Just last night in the plaza a horrible, old hag came out of nowhere and dragged a ten-year-old girl away like an ogre. This woman, apparently the mother of the child, bent the girl's arm behind her back until it nearly broke, the child crying out hysterically in pain. The other children told me today that this mother regularly beats her children. There is no father, as he was killed in an overturned truck. Some of the elders of the village have told me that this child beating has taken on alarming proportions. It is the disease of the soul, an old man said, his eyes full of tears. Times are changed, here as everywhere. A loathsome, palpable darkness seems to me to be stalking us. I hope I'm wrong.

CHAPTER TEN

I AWAKE THIS MORNING WITH SLIGHT TREPIDATION IN THE PIT OF my stomach, an uneasy gnawing upon my soul, though fresh sunlight falls upon my face through the eastern window. Children are on their way to school, and the hoofbeats on the cobblestones tell me the men are off to work in their fields. Pocha is getting ready for the day; I can hear her rattling pots and pans in the kitchen below, while French and German travelers with thick accents order breakfast in Spanish. The walls and ceiling of my room seem ghastly, dirty, abused, holding the lingering, mixed vibrations of a thousand other travelers holed up here over the last five years. Something is wrong.

My hunger this morning is not for food, though I do try to eat eggs and toast in the small restaurant. Pocha knows something is amiss, for I lack the usual morning humor I generally unleash about her stove that does not function and the medium-to-cool shower that is touted as hot. She bends down to remove my plate and quietly inquires: "*¿Hay problemas, Luis?*" Would that I knew, I would tell her. But I only vaguely intuit that something has gone awry, perhaps back home, perhaps here in Peru.

I go to see Carbajal soon after breakfast, arriving in his quiet courtyard to find the wobbly-kneed old man sitting in the sun, his crutches leaning against the stone house, a granddaughter of three upon his lap, and surrounded with the usual pigs, chickens, and sheep. "*Pase adelante, amigo mío. Estuve esperándote.*" (Come in, I've been expecting you.) My mind grapples with the possibility that this shaman with the crooked legs and the laughing face already knows what is wrong. He gently lowers the small girl onto the ground, reaches for his crutches and pulls himself upward, then moves disjointedly into his house.

There is a new seriousness about the way Carbajal handles me this morning. His eyes look down upon the strewn coca leaves on the bedspread; his hands move awkwardly, large-knuckled, arthritic fingers lingering over an erratic leaf, omen of something he hesitates to tell me. Is it Taylor? Is it my mother? Is it about the *Sendero Luminoso*? One leaf, its emerald greenness like no other on the spread, sits miscued and cockeyed—a cipher that only the old man knows how to read. Carbajal's wife with the hatchet face passes by on the way to bring carrot tops to the chickens, and turns her head slowly to look at the leaves. She moves on, head bending down to ease through the doorway. At long last he looks up at me, full-eyed, intent, and intelligent. He speaks.

"*Luis, ¿quién es el amigo latino en Cuzco?*" (Luis, who is the Latin friend in Cuzco?) I remind him that I have a friend called Roberto, a man of spiritual knowledge, an ally, a partner in the new medical clinic we are planning to build here in Ollanta. Carbajal puts away the leaves, eyes downcast, saying nothing.

The bile in my stomach begins to come up into my throat, a slight acidic taste of sickness and death. Now I know that this anxiety, this churning of my emotional self this morning, is related to Roberto. But what level of the man? His relationship with Benito, the shaman of Huasao? His work with building apartments to raise money for the clinic? Or is it something about our relationship? Our friendship? The old man leans back against the headboard of his bed and sighs, then addresses me.

"*Luis, Roberto no es tu amigo. El quiere tu plata en vez de tu amistad. Cuidado.*" (Be careful, Luis, Roberto is after your money.) Carbajal's wife enters and looks at me mournfully. I burn with rage and confusion, my head spins, and I pound my fist into the bed. I implore Carbajal to tell me that it's not true. He shakes his head, the old woman touching my shoulder with her hand lightly and then moving on to the kitchen. In a gentle tone now, like a good father with his son, Carbajal tells me that I must go to Cuzco and get my money from this Roberto.

The ride to Cuzco seems incredibly short, perhaps because I hire an *expreso* taxi, but also in part from my fixation with what I am going to say to the man, this Latino with the smooth tongue. Like an actor, I arrange my lines, going over content before opening night; the script must be delivered unerringly. Were it only ten dollars or a hundred dollars that I had given Roberto, it would be a different script, less severe, almost detached. But it was much more than that. It was close to three thousand dollars that I could ill afford to lose. I remember the trouble he had getting the bills out of the money pouch, the hidden clasps unfamiliar to him. He laughed that day when he came back from the bank and told me the money almost wouldn't come out. The taxi moves swiftly through the afternoon light, tires screaming on the tarmac corners. In my mind I can see Roberto removing my money from the red pouch, slender, brown fingers trying desperately to open it, to get at the crisp, American bills.

He is there, of course, when I get to Cuzco, in his apartment in San Blas. I make polite conversation as he greets me at the courtyard door. I talk, as my script mandates, about trivial things as we walk the one hundred or so paces through dark passageways and through gates to his secluded apartment. Does he know that I have come to confront him? He makes coffee, but before the water is hot enough, I lunge at him with words. Too soon, Ethan, too soon. Stay to the script. But the emotional self rages up, and words that are not mine fly out at him as he stands there by the stove waiting for the kettle to boil.

"Where's the money for the clinic? Why haven't you bought the land? My money was for the down payment. Where's my money, Roberto?" My eyes tear at him with anger. Already my voice is breaking.

It is a strange first defense that he puts up. It is about my loud voice, my shouting, in his house. This must be some Latino custom I have broken. He has struck quickly, for he will not permit a further word unless I address him in a softer, more gentle voice. But this is impossible in my condition. I hate him this moment, for he is denying me my cross-examination. I calm myself with deep breaths, relax my clenched fists, and slowly and coherently ask him again, civily, whether there is any of the money left. He calmly tells me that six hundred of it is in his bank account. The other portions have gone to pay for Rocío's flight back to Seville, as well as a ticket for a Quebec friend of his by the name of Pascal. Both needed money to get home; both had none.

Then he throws his ace. The money, he says, is not my money, but God's money to be used for God's work. Roberto smiles smugly, like some petty thief, I think. This man of higher consciousness, what is he telling me? Is he the perfect teacher for me about my attachment to money? On one level, it's an amazing thing he has done, this declaration that others needed the money more than I, more than the clinic. My mind gropes for the authenticity and integrity of what he is saying. I almost buy it.

I go at him now with passionate words, ignoring his Latino custom of being civil in his own home, hoping to shatter his calm defense.

"You talk about Christ, you talk about shamanism and Benito handing over the reins of Incan wisdom to you. You talk about the lost city of Paititi and going there with your higher consciousness. And I say, bullshit! You don't know crap about purity or spirituality. You're a fucking thief. You're a petty thief, the kind you find in bus stations in Mexico City."

It is this thief-calling that enrages him. Perhaps it is the worst thing to call a Latino man, though looking back on my life I remember an almost identical situation that happened to me in the jungles of Guatemala. A Guatemalan friend of mine named Ricardo Figuerrero, drunk on cheap wine, nearly slipped a switchblade between my ribs when I boldly stood up to him and called him a *borracho*, a drunkard. Latino men are proud about their actions, whether it's stealing money or drinking too much. Often they think they are in the right.

Roberto nearly throws the now-boiling water at me. He feigns the motion—a bluff. But it is there. He seems cornered; the money under his responsibility for the clinic has all but disappeared, and now a friend is calling him a thief. But he calms down and speaks quietly.

"I used the money because two friends needed it at the time. It isn't your money. It isn't even your family's money. It belongs to God. I did what was needed at the time, as I always do. It is my calling to act exactly as I see fit each moment of my life. I will never be any other way. I move in the moment of a mosquito's wing beat. As far as a thief, no, I am anything but a thief. A thief is petty and steals money. I use money, for others. You'll get the money, every penny of it, with interest on it. I'm not a thief and don't you ever call me one. Now get out of my house and leave me."

With these words he turns and walks into his bedroom and I am left there in the kitchen, devastated. Is he right? Is it all God's money and we just get to hold it for a little while? My frazzled mind doesn't know where to alight. Didn't beautiful Rocío hint that she needed money to get home, and did not this Pascal mention one night at the cafe that he might have AIDS and needed to be with his family? Oh God, what have I done? Is there not still money in my wallet?

Roberto is at work in his bedroom, reading. I can see him at his desk. There is integrity in his being, still. Unbelievably, he has the look of someone calm and decent, above reproach. I move toward him to apologize, trying vainly to qualify the statements I have made by asking him what he would have done in my position. It comes off weakly, this mild apologizing, and he is not in a frame of mind to accept it. The damage has been done. I doubted him. He simply says that the friendship has been lost, over money and lack of faith. He does not turn from his writing desk, but speaks slowly and smoothly. "You'll get your money, Ethan; you will get all of it back. And maybe someday you will learn. As of yet you still don't know. Now please leave me."

But I am not through here yet. I tell him I am going to take my books, tapes, pictures, tape recorder, things for the clinic. Without looking at me he says, "Take them, they are still yours." I move about his bedroom taking down pictures, rummaging as quietly as possible through bookshelves for my books. It is painful work. This removal of gifts is symptomatic of my attachment to the material world. I am a small player, I think. I hold back from giving unconditionally. I am sick at taking down these photographs I have taken of places and people around the world. The smiling faces seem to mock me now.

To make matters worse, or better, as the case probably is, I have far too many possessions to carry out easily, gracefully. The trunk I take back is so loaded down with stuff that I strain under its weight and it scrapes the wooden floor. I can barely get it out of the apartment compound, my arms overflow with things that keep slipping out and falling on the ground. I am bent over, hauling, dragging. But finally I am out, to the side street and fresh air. I look unsuccessfully for a taxi, daring not venture too far from my assembled belongings on the stoop lest thieves steal them. How ironic. My mind shrieks with the remembrance of the Latin word

for baggage—*impedimentum*. I am dying from my attachment to these things. And then it's over. I am in a taxi with my things, speeding out of the city with my tail between my legs, heading home.

Returning to Ollanta, night has come, and I walk with Pocha in the moonlight, down through eucalyptus groves beside a brook, close to the railroad station. I choose not to tell her about what has happened today in Cuzco. It is too complicated, too unclear as to whether Roberto is a thief or I am oblivious to what God is trying to teach me about attachment, to money, or friendship, or anything. Pocha's quiet demeanor is comforting; she is full of peace and serenity and I feel healed just standing beside her. We walk silently through the groves on a path, across patches of moonlight and leafy silhouettes of branches overhead, like latticework of fine lace. Cicadas sing in the forest, a cow moans softly in a dark barn close by. There are crickets along the path, their serenade melting into the sound of rushing glacial waters on smooth stones in the riverbed.

We move quietly to a place she seems to know. She stops, and sits upon a huge flat stone, like a table. It is beautiful in the forest, damp and sweet with the fragrance of bougainvillea and other vines that have released their scents into the night. Quietly, Pocha asks me if I know the Lord's Prayer. I tell her that I do, in English. She laughs gently and asks if I could follow her in Spanish. I nod my head and we begin. All the times I have mumbled the words, from first grade with my head bent down on the ill-smelling, shellacked desks of elementary school to locker-room ordeals where the coach asks the boys to pray for victory, this prayer has had little or no effect on me. But here in the forest, in Spanish of all things, the words come to life and mingle with the stream and the cicadas and a lone bird's sweet song. We rise, silhouettes falling upon us from the branches above, and walk quietly home. The slow, gentle pace of one foot after another on the earthen trail is comforting.

Today is rainy and I want to hide away in my room. It has been a trying day, the culmination of many things that have been building up within me for many months. They are neither good things nor bad things. They are the things that have happened. I look again at my life and sigh. The children often ask me why it is that I sigh, and I tell them that my sighing has many meanings. Sometimes the sigh is from a deep satisfaction, other times the sigh reflects the exhaustive nature of my searching, my slow progress upon the path. I have opened myself so much to so many things these long months here that today my heart seems wounded and ripped, the aura around it torn and frayed like some blown-up balloon. This journey has taken its toll on me in the speed and intensity in which it has happened. I don't think I've ever experienced so much, so fast, so poignantly. I have brought it on myself, praying innumerable times for an opening up of my senses and my consciousness, a reunion with my true spiritual self. Now the gates have opened and flooded my being.

Children stand outside my window and call in their plaintive voices, Luis, Luis, come play, come play. Can it be that I am through with playing, that I am finished here? Is it time to go? I lose my temper and run down the stairs like an ogre and chase them away. It is the first time I have done this, and Pocha comes to me and brings me into her kitchen to hold me, as she soothes my trembling like a mother who knows what is happening inside her child. They mean no harm, she says. I return to my room and lie quietly all day with shallow breathing. I feel naked. What good

is this questing if it leads me into disarray and anger? Perhaps I need the ordinary life like everyone else seems to find: a life that is predictable, convenient, material, and safe.

In the afternoon the rain stops and the sun emerges. Though it is Sunday, a few families are out in their *chacras* putting manure on their fields. They wave to me everywhere I go, and I back at them. I wander to some grottos where I know no one will be, seeking the views of snowy La Verónica in the late-afternoon sunshine. I feel like crying, like praying out loud for the mistakes I have made, for the sins I have committed, none of which seem to have a name.

Soon I come to a series of hidden stone terraces where ferns and succulent plants abound, and where no animals have disturbed the lovely flowers growing out of the stone crevices. My eyes focus on a cluster of pristine white lilies arching their slender, green necks out of a cleft in the stonework. I move closer, drawn like a magnet.

These are the lilies of the fields. In the Bible, Christ said, "Consider the lilies of the fields, for they toil not, nor do they spin. Yet I say to you that not even Solomon in all his glory was arrayed like one of them." I move in and lightly cup a lily in my two hands, and tears fall upon the staman and the soft insides of white and pale gold. A gentle wind from off the snow peaks caresses my cheeks like a kiss. The air is pungent with these aromas of wildflowers and sweet-scented mosses; it reminds me of cool church anterooms where we children were allowed to take home a potted flower at Eastertime. I move about the grotto as if it were my old room in Connecticut and I have just returned after years of wandering. So here it is, I think, right here, right here; I have come home again.

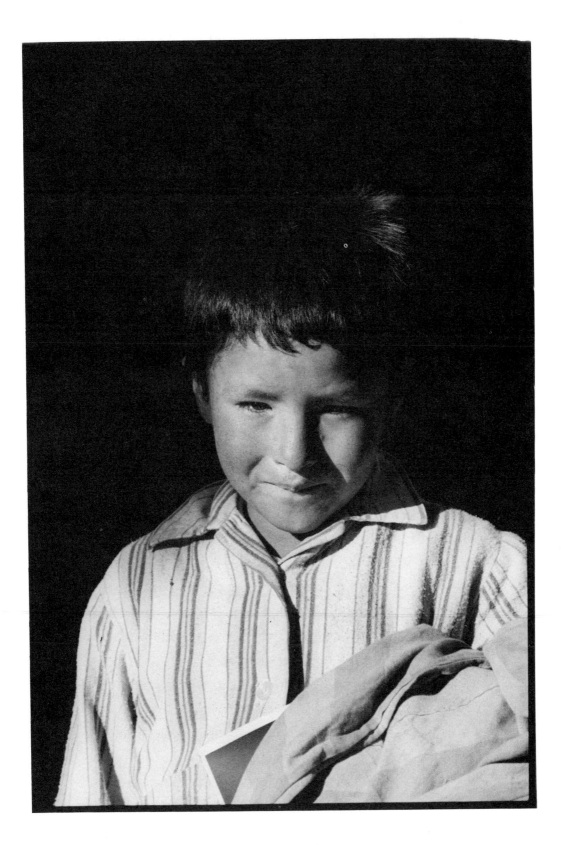

Two small boys find me and advance quietly on the soft mosses, standing behind me until I sense their presence. I turn and behold their dear, open faces, faces as unlined and unworried as the pure white insides of the lilies. They are in rags and smiling. I do not know these two boys, I have never seen them before. I want to ask them, who are you, what are your names? But there is no reason. Their serenity and peacefulness are their names, their faces are their names. I lightly touch them on the heads, my hands in slow motion before me, the boys unafraid. They stand so quietly, waiting for something, yet I know not what.

My mind goes blank, no thoughts. My hand slowly unleashes my daypack. It slides comfortably down my shoulder, striking the earth with a soft thud. No mind still, just hands opening the pack and feeling. For what? I do not know. I vaguely remember coming out of the pension with the pack, not knowing its contents or even why I was taking it. And then my hands feel the fuzzy cover of a tennis ball. It is the last ball I have, saved for some special occasion. I remember, and pull it out; the boys' eyes widen and brighten. It is a new, bright yellow tennis ball, bought long months ago from a drugstore on the green in Washington, Connecticut, with a promise of a gift to some child in South America. And I hold it a few seconds, feeling it, and then lightly toss it to them. They both hold onto it, four hands now covering it. Their eyes are on me, a pleading look, though not covetous. May we play with it? Is it real? Are we here? Yes, yes, yes, it's all true, we are here, and the ball is for you, forever.

We three move three, four, five paces backwards like dancers and softly toss the ball to each other. Instantly I feel as though a great weight has been lifted off me. I burst into uncontrollable laughing and crying, a whooping and a hollering, a giddiness throughout my whole body. The boys seem not to think I'm strange, but just right. I take the ball, cock my body back, and heave it with all my might into the pink-orange sky of twilight, where it arcs and stops, then falls into the four outstretched, cupped hands. It is caught.

I walk with the two little boys out of the grotto and toward town, the lilies swaying slightly in the wan light of dusk. We walk hand in hand in silence along the field's border, toward the old grandfather who awaits his grandsons' return. This old man, large boned and sturdy like the root of a massive tree, stands patiently watching, waiting, as we three approach. He wears an old hat and his clothes are worn and frayed, but his being and his posture are proud and strong after all these years of living. He smiles and offers me his large, coarse hand, and his eyes accept me. For surely he, too, has moved with the stirrings and the hastenings of the seasons and the pull upon his soul from a million different invisible callings. Here he is, standing at the edge of the fields, at the end of his long life. His smile and kind demeanor seem to say, it's okay Ethan. Another step along the long, long road of our lives. I sigh and, giving the old man a strong hug around his broad shoulders, look down at the brown earth with its sprouting, green shoots of corn; and we four walk quietly across the *pampa* back to town.

◆

I leave Ollanta soon after that day. My time there has come to an end, as does everything in life. Seasons have changed from dry to wet, the corn is up and green, and children tug at my fingers to join with their families for *choclo con queso*, fresh corn with goat's cheese. Yes, I go, I go until the very end of the last day when the four-o'clock bus departs the town plaza and winds its way over the spine of the Andes to Cuzco and my awaiting flight home to America. I remember the last few minutes of that day, the long

embrace of Pocha and sweet kisses upon the face of Carlitos, now able to say my name, and the walk with my bags to the plaza, telltale signs that this time it is for good. I am going.

Old mothers and grandmothers with toothless grins break through conventionality and embrace me, kiss me full upon the cheeks. Teenage boys, so full of maleness, melt and come close and hold my hand for long seconds. Dare we embrace? No, but the hand is held. Come back, Luis, come back. The bus horn honks and I turn and walk a few awkward steps backward toward the bus, looking at the mountains and the Indians and the faces that have been in my eyes and heart all these months.

For a few brief moments, I have lived in a small valley in a place called Peru, a village called Ollantaytambo, where a thousand hearts took me in and loved me, made me stronger and more whole. A little three-year-old niece of my baker friends touchs my legs. Are you going? she asks. Cristina holds me tightly and lovingly to her bosom. Alberto, the strong husband of the family, extends his hand to mine and his whole being floods into me. Come back, he says, come back always and be part of our family. You are family, Luis. *"Tú eres familia."*

Journey to Ollantaytambo was designed and typeset in Bembo
by Quad Left Graphics.

It was printed on Finch Opaque, an acid-free paper,
by Hamilton Printing.